ROSA RUGOSA

ROSA RUGOSA

Suzanne Verrier

Photographs by Charles Steinhacker

CAPABILITY'S BOOKS

Deer Park, Wisconsin

Front cover photograph   Back cover photograph
'Martin Frobisher'   Fall foliage of
                                   'Fru Dagmar Hastrup'

Text copyright © 1991 by Suzanne Verrier

Foreword copyright © 1991 by Henry Mitchell

Photographs copyright © 1991 by Charles Steinhacker

First edition

91 92 93 94 95 5 4 3 2 1

Library of Congress Catalog Card Number: 91–72462
Library of Congress Cataloging-in-Publication data is available.

ISBN: 0–913643–07–6

Design and production by Stanton Publication Services, Inc.

Printed in Hong Kong

PUBLISHED BY

Capability's Books, Inc.
2379 Highway 46
Deer Park, WI 54007 USA

(715) 269–5346

Capability's Books and colophon are trademarks
of Capability's Books, Inc.

I dedicate this book to my gardens which have taught me so many truths.

My sincerest gratitude is extended to the folowing:

Lynn Collicutt, Bill Vanderkruk, Bob Osborne, Henry Mitchell, Nicholas Weber, Kristen Gilbertson, Paulette Rickard, Joseph Schraven, Beverly Dobson, Roger Vick, Paul Olsen, Lily Shohan, Mike Lowe, Pamela Lord, Trevor Cole, Dr. Eon Ogilvie, and to many other helpful and knowledgeable people for their very valuable assistance.

Contents

Foreword

No PERFUME of any kind surpasses the scent of some rugosa roses, such as 'Roseraie de l'Haÿ', 'Mrs. Anthony Waterer', and 'Hansa', and even those that are less powerfully fragrant, such as 'Agnes' or 'Sarah Van Fleet' or 'Sir Thomas Lipton' are still far sweeter than most flowers.

Furthermore, the wrinkled leaves of this group of roses are ornamental and for the most part healthy, and the plants have the exceptional merit of being more at home in the North than the South.

It is strange that so little has been written about them. Usually they are left to bring up the caboose in the rose world, and one might get the impression that they are poor relations of the queen of flowers.

But it is far otherwise. Some of the rugosas, not all, bloom off and on through the summer and early fall. In general they never get mildew and rarely blackspot, and if they do, it does not affect their abundant flowering.

The gardening world will welcome a book which is devoted entirely to these roses, and which provides more detailed comment than the gardener can usually find.

The author observes she has dropped 'Sir Thomas Lipton', a poor doer with her, and that is a good warning for gardeners of the far North. But in the South, where some rugosas falter, 'Sir Thomas Lipton' excels. On the Tennessee-Mississippi border, for example, that rose gets some blackspot in summer and produces flowers steadily, but the hot-weather blooms are shapeless. And yet at the end of April, 'Sir Thomas Lipton' is solid with white roses of the quality of old formal camellias, so it should not lightly be cast out.

Even a small garden such as my own can hold several rugosa roses—I have grown eight varieties and every one a winner.

The chief danger of this book is that the gardener will be tempted to grow every rose mentioned in it, but then gardeners have braved worse dangers in their day and have fallen into less enchanting temptations. It is possible, after all, that one does not need so much lawn?

HENRY MITCHELL

Introduction

ASK THE IMPOSSIBLE and the answer is: grow rugosas. If you live in an area where temperatures plummet to below zero, you can have thriving roses, roses that do not need to be pampered by rose cones or tipped over and buried under a protective layer of soil in order to survive the winter. Rugosas are exceedingly hardy. They are also disease resistant, pest resistant, wind and salt tolerant, defiant of urban pollution, and vigorous. A planting of rugosas will clothe bare banks or form impenetrable hedges in only a few years' time. Grow rugosas and you will enjoy fragrant flowers, not once, but throughout the season. Choose single blooms, semi-doubles, or many-petaled doubles; large blossoms or small ones; solitary roses held aloft one by one or multitudes in tightly packed clusters; blossoms of soft pink, vivid pink, lilac-pink, crimson, rich purple-crimson, bold scarlet, startlingly pure white, white blushed with pink, or creamy yellow. A rugosa can be found to match any garden color scheme, any whim of individual taste. From colorful blossoms in spring, summer, and fall to attractive canes free to catch the new snowfall in winter, from healthy green leaves to exciting fall foliage color, rugosas are year-round winners. These are roses ideally suited to the demands of today's gardens and gardeners.

Each year, more and more gardeners discover the attributes of *Rosa rugosa* and its hybrids. As rugosas gain popularity, the number of available varieties is increasing. The importance of these roses is recognized. Historically, this group has contributed to some of the most prestigious modern rose breeding programs. *R. rugosa* is a strong and prolific parent. From Germany, Kordes' *R. kordesii* (derived from rugosa stock) is one of the most important parents in the realm of hardy roses. England's David Austin has used rugosa hybrids in the breeding of some of his popular English roses. The Canadian Explorer series developed by Felicitas Svedja relies heavily upon the hardy rugosas. In the past few decades, more noteworthy rugosas have originated in Canada than in any other part of the world. The continuing Canadian commitment to hardy high-performance roses enriches gardens wherever roses are grown. In the future, new varieties will reach the market from Germany and from the Far East, the original home of *R. rugosa* where it has been cultivated for nearly a millennium.

Each age has its own tastes, fashions, and favored plants. Although rugosas are now increasing in popularity, these roses have had an uneven albeit interesting history. For centuries rugosas flourished in Korea, Japan, and China before being transported to England in the late-eighteenth century. One is struck by the lack of enthusiasm with which the Europeans greeted the rugosas. Little excitement was caused by their introduction and the immediate response was criticism citing coarseness, excessive vigor, and lack of refinement. No mention was given to the plants' disease resistance, hardiness, or strong pleasing fragrance. Most extraordinary of all, no one praised the repeat bloom of rugosas; repeat flowering is a trait almost unknown among other species roses. Perhaps these unique roses were too practical for a time in European history when fussiness reigned. Or, perhaps, rugosas arrived in the wrong country; England's mild and temperate climate has always freed gardeners from placing major emphasis on plant hardiness.

A century passed before major hybridizing began. Although Paul and others developed varieties in England, the first major surge of rugosa hybridizing began in colder countries: America, France, and Germany. The late 1800s and early 1900s saw exciting new rugosa hybrids being developed by Gravereaux and Cochet-Cochet in France and by Kaufmann and Müller in Germany. North Americans more quickly recognized the strengths of *R. rugosa*. Here, too, development began at the turn of the century though rugosas had only recently reached America, in 1872, arriving not from Europe like most other rose species but instead directly from the Far East. Hybridizers active in America and Canada were Carmen, Van Fleet, and Budd; later, Skinner, Saunders, and Hansen.

These early enthusiasts crossed *R. rugosa* with hybrid teas, damascenas, floribundas, hybrid perpetuals, ramblers, climbing teas, polyanthas, as well as with other species roses. Sadly, many of these interesting crosses have disappeared from commerce despite the success of *R. rugosa*. Hardy and adaptable to varied conditions, the species quickly naturalized around the world.

In Maine, wild rugosas have naturalized to the extent that *Rosa rugosa* is regarded as the "wild beach rose." As a native of

Maine, one who has always been fascinated by these free-spirited shrubs, and as a nursery person and garden designer, my intent has long been to popularize the garden uses of rugosas. When I first offered rugosas for sale, customers continued to demand hybrid teas and floribundas, even though these were frequently killed in our winter climate. Time progressed and the attributes of hardiness and disease resistance have won the day; rugosas now represent the largest portion of my rose sales. As plants were sent to mail-order customers across the country, I was curious to observe many leaving for mild California gardens. Inquiries revealed that West Coast gardeners were using rugosas to solve pest and disease problems. With so many advantages, rugosas hold different benefits for different gardeners. Having so much to offer, they should never again be greeted without enthusiasm. This book continues my quest.

What follows is a collection of rugosas and rugosa hybrids, an overview of the realm and reaches of this exciting group of roses. The first section contains descriptions and photographs of rugosas available to gardeners through commercial sources. Unfortunately, for reasons of distance or weather, not all could be captured on film. The descriptions note height and spread, parentage (seed parent followed by pollen parent), and origin (hybridizer, country and date of introduction). Boldface type in the parentage line indicates that the parent is a rugosa and alerts the reader to a separate entry for that rose. Following the first section are brief chapters on the cultivation and design uses of *R. rugosa* and its hybrids. The second section of this book focuses on obscure rugosas – historically important hybrids and interesting crosses; these are not available to the home gardener. Hopefully, the rugosas which have strayed from commerce remain in cultivation, for these roses from the past hold promise for tomorrow's gardens. Who can predict where the whims of rose breeders and the demands of consumers will lead if interest in lost roses is aroused? The words precede, accompany, and follow but the roses speak plainly for themselves. May you enjoy them. May they soon grow in your garden.

ROSA RUGOSA

R. RUGOSA 'ALBA'

Rugosas for the Home Gardener

Rosa rugosa

NATIVE TO NORTHEASTERN ASIA, this rose species was carried to Europe and North America as well as to other parts of the world. So hardy, so successful in adaptation, *Rosa rugosa* has freely naturalized and is often mistaken as a native species. A precise description of the true species is difficult because, unlike most other rose species, *R. rugosa* is variable from seed: seedlings may or may not exactly resemble the parent species rose. Variations of form occur naturally. With this difficulty in mind, a general description of *R. rugosa* would include the following traits. Described by many as the hardiest of all roses, this rose will survive the frigid temperatures of zone 2, minus 50 to minus 40 degrees Fahrenheit. Depending on soil conditions, it can reach a height varying from three to over six feet. The thick stems are exceedingly prickly. The large, elliptically shaped, deeply veined leaves are crinkled or wrinkled ("rugose"). Rugosa leaves are a rich, healthy shade of dark green; the golden-yellow autumnal shades are striking. Blossoms are recurrent: blooms appear in early spring and continue into the fall. Flowers, which open from attractive long-pointed buds, are pink to crimson and, depending on the form, may be single or double, solitary or held in clusters. *R. rugosa* is exceedingly fragrant. Its large fruits, or hips, are smooth and round, almost crab apple-like in form.

In addition to the two most common forms described below, 'Alba' and 'Rubra', other botanical names denote specific variations from the basic species: *R. r. chamissoniana*, almost thornless; *R. r.* 'Rosea', single pink blossoms; *R. r.* 'Plena', double colored blossoms; *R. r.* 'Albo-plena', white double blossoms.

R. rugosa 'Alba'
6' x 6'
Introduced mid- to late-19th century

This naturally occurring form of *R. rugosa* displays the whitest of white, large fragrant single blossoms with a poppy-like quality and cream-colored stamens. The buds are long, elegant, and the palest blush pink. Large, glossy, healthy, deep green foliage sets off consistent clusters of blooms and large orange hips. The growth of *R. rugosa* 'Alba' is denser and more decorative than that of *R. r.* 'Rubra', making 'Alba' a better subject in the garden. It is such a beautiful shrub that I'm not sure any of the white hybrids can really better its appeal.

R. RUGOSA 'RUBRA'

R. rugosa 'Rubra'
6′ x 6′
Introduced to England, circa 1796

R. rugosa 'Rubra' is the red-flowering form of R. rugosa. This form and the true species can easily be, and frequently are, confused; in many cases, it is R. rugosa 'Rubra' that is available in nurseries, not the true species plant. R. rugosa 'Rubra' is recurrent and the large blossoms are very deep pink with purple overtones. Cream-colored stamens. The strong fragrance is readily carried on a breeze and the large hips are orange-scarlet. Foliage is bright green, crinkled and glossy with good fall color. This shrub suckers readily, which can be an advantage or a disadvantage depending upon placement. (Also known as R. rugosa 'Atropurpurea'.)

AGNES

Agnes

5′ x 5′

R. rugosa x *R. foetida* 'Persiana'
Saunders, Canada, 1922

'Agnes' boasts pale, creamy yellow, fully double blossoms that are unusual among the rugosas. Although sometimes listed as recurrent, in my experience this rose will not produce flowers after a fairly profuse early summer flowering. The dense foliage is very dark green and heavily crinkled. While there are those who consider these curious leaves to be an attribute, to me the foliage always appears diseased or blighted.

If you must have a yellow rugosa, 'Agnes' would be a good choice. Two strong recommendations for this shrub are its hardiness and the scent of its uncommon blossoms.

Alice Aldrich

R. rugosa x 'Caroline de Sansal' (Hybrid Perpetual)
Lovett, USA, 1901

This rugosa variety bears large, double, bright clear-pink flowers that are recurrent. Not widely grown worldwide, this rose appears to be available only in the U.S., where it was originally introduced by the Conard & Jones nursery (or as known today, the Conard-Pyle Company).

Amélie Gravereaux

5′ x 5′

[('Général Jacqueminot' (Hybrid Perpetual) x 'Maréchal Niel' (Noisette)] x **'Conrad Ferdinand Meyer'**
Gravereaux, France, 1903

A hybrid perpetual cross noisette crossed with a hybrid rugosa. Although the rugosa genes are quite diluted in this hybrid, strong rugosa affinities appear especially in the deep green rugose foliage. Possessing good fragrance, the double flowers are a medium purple-crimson shade. A vigorous shrub, well armed with prickles. Recurrent. It is interesting to note that this rose was hybridized by Jules Gravereaux, an owner of the famous French department store Bon Marché, who retired and created the equally famous garden La Roseraie de l'Haÿ les-Roses at the turn of the century. Gravereaux sought to amass the most extensive rose collection in the world. His love of roses led from collecting to hybridizing; 'Rose à Parfum de l'Haÿ' was another of his many rugosa hybrids.

Ann Endt

R. rugosa x *R. foliolosa*
Nobbs, New Zealand, 1978

This is an interesting hybrid of *R. rugosa*, originating from the Far East, and *R. foliolosa*, a native of the southern prairies of the United States. These two species are similar in some ways, yet very different.

'Ann Endt', a product of New Zealand rose hybridizers, is neither widely available nor well documented. The blossom is deep crimson and single which is predictable since both parents are single roses. The cinnamon scent, not characteristic of the rugosas, is probably attributable to *R. foliolosa*. Descriptions of the foliage note that it is small; however, curiously, no mention is made of it being narrow, a typical trait of foliolosa foliage. 'Ann Endt' may be available in New Zealand.

Arnold (Arnoldiana)

4' x 4'
R. rugosa x 'Général Jacqueminot' (Hybrid Perpetual)
Dawson, USA, 1893

Five-petaled, crinkled, bright deep pink blossoms with some repeat bloom. A vigorous shrub with deep green foliage, 'Arnold' reflects its rugosa parentage.

Basye's Purple

3' x 3'
R. foliolosa x **R. rugosa** 'Rubra'
Basye, USA, 1980

Single, 2½-inch, dark purple blossoms with a fruity fragrance. Repeat bloom. Dark green rugose foliage and very thorny purple canes. 'Basye's Purple' is upright in growth with some suckering. Hardy. Does not set hips of any significant number. Interestingly, Dr. Basye's rose breeding efforts in Texas seek hardy hybrids with drought tolerance.

Belle Poitevine

5' x 5'
Parentage unknown
Bruant, France, 1894

The four-inch blossoms are flat and semi-double to double in form. The color of the blooms is almost identical to the soft pink of hollyhock mallow (*Malva moschata*) and combines nicely with the pale cream-colored stamens. Fresh light fragrance, repeat blooms and occasional scarlet hips. The form and size of the blossoms play against the handsome mid-green rugose foliage. 'Belle Poitevine' is dense growing and makes a very attractive hedge rose in addition to being an excellent garden variety. The absence of any lavender tones in the blossoms and the open form of the blooms are two traits that should strengthen its importance among the rugosas. Oddly, the parentage of this popular rose seems to have escaped historical record.

BELLE POITEVINE

Big John (See 'Galleria'.)

Blanc Double de Coubert
5′ x 4′
R. rugosa x 'Sombreuil' (Climbing Tea)
Cochet-Cochet, France, 1892

Loosely double, snow white blossoms with a strong fragrance. Recurrent bloom but sets only a few hips. The dark shiny green dense foliage is average size for the rugosas. 'Blanc Double de Coubert' retains attractive healthy foliage throughout the season and shows good fall color. This was one of the first rugosas to gain popularity and deservedly so. In *Roses for English Gardens*, Gertrude Jekyll describes 'Blanc Double de Coubert' as the "whitest rose of any known" and "one of the best of roses," high praise from a most discerning gardener.

Calocarpa (*R. x calocarpa*)
5′ x 5′
R. rugosa x *R. chinensis*
Bruant, France, 1895

Because *R. x calocarpa*, a hybrid from the 19th century, has only recently returned to commerce, there is disagreement concerning its ability to rebloom. I have several plants, from two sources, and none are recurrent. Large, single, deep lilac-pink blossoms with a prominent center of yellow stamens. Fragrant flowers precede small orange-scarlet hips. Foliage is attractive and elongated but rugose in character. More graceful in growth with long arching canes and less dense in form than other

BELLE POITEVINE

BLANC DOUBLE DE COUBERT

11

CALOCARPA

CALOCARPA

rugosas. *R. x calocarpa* with its subtle appeal will always have a place in my garden, most particularly for the many seedling crosses it produces each season.

Carmen
4′ x 4′
R. rugosa x 'Princesse de Béarn' (Hybrid Perpetual)
Lambert, Germany, 1907

Large, single, deep crimson blossoms with wavy crinkled petals. The fragrant flowers, having prominent pale yellow stamens, are borne in clusters. Deep green foliage and dense growth. Only some repeat flowering.

Carmenetta (*R. x rubrosa*)
7′ x 9′
R. rubrifolia x **R. rugosa**
Central Experimental Farm, Canada, 1923

Unusual for inheriting so little influence from its rugosa parent, 'Carmenetta' mostly resembles its rubrifolia parent in its glaucous-reddish foliage and red canes. Like rubrifolia blossoms, those of this cross are single, pale pink, borne in clusters, non-recurrent, and lightly fragrant. Developed in Canada, this is a very hardy rose, as one might expect. The tall growth is arching and spreading.

Charles Albanel
1′ x 3′
'Souvenir de Philémon Cochet' x ?
Svejda, Canada, 1982

The medium crimson blossoms are double, measure three inches across, and contain about 20 petals. The fragrant flowers of 'Charles Albanel' are borne in clusters and repeat throughout the summer. This hardy shrub has yellow-green rugose foliage that is admirably disease resistant. These attributes, and the trait of low-spreading growth, make this rose a useful ground cover rose.

Conrad Ferdinand Meyer

6' x 5'

['Gloire de Dijon' (Cl. Tea) x 'Duc de Rohan' (Centifolia)]
x 'Germanica'
Müller, Germany, 1899

This shrub illustrates the strength of rugosa genes. With tea, bourbon and centifolia influences combined, it is still quite evident that 'Conrad Ferdinand Meyer' has rugosa in its breeding. The fragrance is rich, strong, and appropriate to the decisive character of this shrub. 'Conrad Ferdinand Meyer' has a vigorous angular growth and large foliage that is somewhat modern but still appears rugose. The large recurrent blossoms are an appealing pink shade and resemble an exaggerated hybrid tea rose. Because of its rigid form of growth, this rose is best planted behind lower roses or at the back of a border.

Corylus

3' x 3'

R. rugosa x R. nitida
Le Rougetel, England, 1988

Hazel Le Rougetel in her book A Heritage of Roses tells of the circumstances surrounding her "only rose creation," an encouragement to any-would-be rose hybridizer. I have not grown this rose but am resolved to order it promptly from England since I am very partial to species crosses and believe in supporting independent and amateur breeders.

The flowers are described by Hazel Le Rougetel as a silvery medium pink, single, and fragrant. A special feature is the dense, small, and elongated foliage which turns gold and tawny red in the fall. There is also a good crop of bright scarlet hips.

Culverbrae

5' x 4'

'Scabrosa' x 'Francine' (Hybrid Tea)
Gobbee, England, 1973

The attraction of 'Culverbrae' is its large, very double blossoms, measuring up to four inches across. These are crimson-purple, very fragrant, and somewhat recurrent.

I cannot help wondering why 'Francine', the pollen parent, disappeared from commerce so quickly; less than two decades have passed since this cross was made. 'Culverbrae' may hold a clue. In addition to modern uncrinkled foliage, 'Culverbrae' inherited a weakness to mildew. Perhaps 'Francine' deserved to vanish?

Dart's Dash

4' x 4'

R. rugosa hybrid
Darthuis Nursery, Holland, Date unknown

A large-flowered, deep to medium purple-crimson rose. The semi-double blossoms have a strong sweet perfume and are followed by a good display of large hips. Dark green foliage and dense growth make this rose useful as a ground cover. Exhibits hardiness. 'Dart's Dash' repeats well throughout the summer.

CONRAD FERDINAND MEYER

15

Dart's Defender (*R. nitida* 'Defender')
R. nitida x **'Hansa'**
Darthuis Nursery, Holland, 1971

Violet-pink single blossoms and shiny foliage. Vigorous growth. Suitable for covering banks.

David Thompson
4′ x 4′
('Schneezwerg' x **'Fru Dagmar Hastrup')**
x unknown seedling
Canadian Explorer Series, Canada, 1979

The seed parent 'Schneezwerg' influences the small foliage and the dimensions of 'David Thompson'. The blossoms are deep pinkish-crimson, neither a clean color nor one that is easy to use in a planting scheme. They are about 2¾ inches across, are somewhere between semi-double and double, and appear consistently throughout the summer. The foliage is mid-green with some yellow-green tones that seem to work against, rather than enhance, the color of the blossoms. Quite obviously, 'David Thompson' is not one of my favorites but I am beginning to appreciate this shrub more as it is rarely without blossoms.

DAVID THOMPSON

Delicata
4′ x 3′
Parentage unknown
Cooling, USA, 1898

Very pretty papery lilac-pink semi-double blossoms with a strong and delightful fragrance. The foliage is good and typically rugose in character. The hips are large and scarlet-orange, frequently displayed along with later blossoms from midsummer through early fall. This hybrid rugosa is frequently criticized for its lack of vigor and its uneven growth habits but I have not found this to be true in my gardens. It is accepting of various conditions

Delicata

including dampness, and although it is narrow rather than spreading, the growth is dense, almost mounded in form. 'Delicata' stays predictably within bounds and certainly has its applications in garden designs.

Dr. Eckener

8' x 6'
'Golden Emblem' x unknown *R. rugosa*
Berger, Germany, 1930

Was the seed parent the hybrid tea introduced as 'Golden Emblem' in 1917, or the climbing hybrid tea of the same name introduced in 1927? Regardless of the parent's type, it was the source of the appealing pale yellow, copper-tinted flowers of 'Dr. Eckener'.

A climbing hybrid tea lineage might explain why this rose is so tall. Generally its size is only a problem in more temperate areas. In Maine, severe winters limit its growth. In cold climates, winter dieback occurs.

Fragrant and recurrent. All in all, 'Dr. Eckener' is another yellow rugosa that probably would not have continued in commerce were it not for the unique color of its blossoms. The growth is coarse, ungracefully filled with fearsome thorns. Foliage is sparse.

DELICATA

Fimbriata

4′ x 4′

R. rugosa x 'Mme. Alfred Carrière' (Noisette)
Morlet, France, 1891

Having only recently acquired 'Fimbriata' and being not at all fond of the Grootendorst roses, I was predisposed to dislike this little fringed rose. But 'Fimbriata' was a pleasant surprise. Delicately frilled small white blossoms, blushed with pale pink and beautifully displayed against dense bright green foliage, won this rose an undisputed spot at the front of its bed. Fragrant and recurrent with some hips, all 'Fimbriata' needed to do was prove its hardiness, which it has. Also known as 'Dianthiflora'.

F. J. Grootendorst

F. J. Grootendorst
5′ x 4′

R. rugosa 'Rubra' x 'Mme. Norbert Levavasseur' (Polyantha)
de Goey, Holland, 1918

Grootendorst Supreme. 4 ft. Grootendorst, Holland, 1936.
Deep crimson red.
Pink Grootendorst. 4 ft. Grootendorst, Holland, 1923. Bright
mid-pink.
White Grootendorst. 4 ft. Eddy, USA, 1962. White with light fra-
grance.

'Grootendorst Supreme' and 'Pink Grootendorst' are sports of
the original 'F. J. Grootendorst'. 'White Grootendorst' is a sport
of 'Pink Grootendorst'. 'Grootendorst Supreme' has more deeply
colored flowers than the crimson blossoms of 'F. J. Grootendorst'. All have tight clusters of small fringed blooms and little
or no perceptible fragrance. The leaves are small and tend toward yellow-green. The rigid growth is taller than wide, making
these roses appropriate to be grown as pillar roses. The Grootendorsts all bloom heavily and repeatedly. Here the attributes end.

Despite the above description I find little to admire in these
shrubs which are peculiarly not rose-like. The growth is
ungraceful and the crowded blossoms do not have any particular beauty or character. The Grootendorsts all tend to attract pests and lack the disease resistance of most rugosas.
Writing of another rose, Graham Stuart Thomas spoke of it as
"soulless." The Grootendorsts might also be described as
"soulless."

Flamingo
3′ x 3′

R. rugosa x 'White Wings' (Hybrid Tea)
Howard, USA, 1956

This shrub with pronounced rugose tendencies is a flamingo
pink version of 'White Wings'. 'Flamingo' is an instance in which
an unlikely cross has created a lovely rose. The blossoms are
single, deep pink with dark red stamens, recurrent, and fragrant. Unfortunately, 'Flamingo' is not hardy in colder climates;
it is best suited for zones 6 and up.

Fru Dagmar Hastrup

4′ x 4′

R. rugosa seedling

Hastrup, Denmark, 1914

Very delicate clear pale pink blossoms, frequently veined with a deeper pink. The large single fragrant flowers and large scarlet hips are attractively oversized for this somewhat diminutive rugosa. However, the combination is very pleasing and 'Fru Dagmar Hastrup' ranks as a classic among the rugosas. The foliage is a deep dark glossy green and mid-sized. Because of its size and density of growth, this rose is an excellent lower hedging shrub as well as a good garden subject. I find that 'Fru Dagmar Hastrup' varies in size from source to source and is usually larger on its own roots than on an understock.

Sometimes listed as 'Frau Dagmar Hartopp'; however, "the Fru" is Danish, not German. 'Fru Dagmar Hastrup' is correct.

Galleria

4′ x 4′

'The Duke' (Hybrid Tea) x **'Hansa'**

Weddle, USA, 1990

Because I had received a very positive endorsement for this rose from a Canadian rose grower, I've placed 'Galleria' on my "must order" list. 'Galleria' is described in rose catalogs as having very large silvery-pink blossoms that start out somewhat cupped and open to a loosely semi-double flower. Very fragrant with good repeat bloom. Vigorous upright open growth with large foliage and very thorny canes. Bearing a resemblance to the rugosa hy-

FRU DAGMAR HASTRUP

22

Fru Dagmar Hastrup

23

brid 'Robusta' and sharing its tendency to blackspot, the positive attributes of 'Galleria' purportedly outweigh this affliction.

('Galleria' was formerly listed under the variety name 'Big John'.)

George Will

4' x 4'

(**R. rugosa** x R. acicularis) x ?
Skinner, Canada, 1939

Large, barely double, deep lilac-pink blossoms that open flat. The blooms are borne in clusters and emit the fragrance of cloves. The canes are slender, resembling those of R. acicularis, but the small foliage is rugose in character. 'George Will' is recurrent and reliably hardy. A gardener's bulletin from Saskatchewan refers to this rose as an "old reliable."

'Grootendorst Supreme'

(See 'F. J. Grootendorst'.)

Hansa

7' x 7'

Parentage unknown
Schaum and Van Tol, Holland, 1905

'Hansa', a particularly nice specimen plant, is a tall-growing, vase-shaped shrub, growing as wide as it is tall. The blossoms are large, double, and deep vibrant purple, crimson. Recurrent with excellent rebloom in the fall. A strong fragrance, reminiscent of

Hansa

HENRY HUDSON

cloves, permeates the air around this shrub. 'Hansa' sets a heavy crop of large scarlet hips and has dark green rugose foliage with attractive fall color. Having excellent vigor, disease resistance and good rebloom, and providing plenty of return for little effort, this rose is recommended for beginning gardeners. 'Hansa' is also a solid choice for a tall rose hedge.

Harvest Home
5′ x 5′
'Scabrosa' x ?
Spicer, England, 1979

Not an extensively grown rugosa, 'Harvest Home' is apparently available only through English and Swiss nurseries. Semi-double flowers of a mauve-pink shade. The large size (4½ inches across) and shallow-cupped form of its blossoms would seem to imitate those of its seed parent. The growth is bushy and the light green foliage has rugose tendencies. 'Harvest Home' blossoms vigorously early in the summer with some repeat bloom.

Henry Hudson
4′ x 3′
'Schneezwerg' seedling
Svejda, Canadian Explorer Series, Canada, 1976

The blossoms are white, about 2½ inches across and semi-double. They open flat with an attractive center of yellow stamens. In cooler weather the blooms show a blush of pink but for most of the summer they are white. The buds are deep pink and rounded, unusual for a rugosa. This shrub repeats often throughout the summer, and the blossoms have the spicy fragrance of cloves. Small to mid-size, deeply crinkled leaves. The flat blossoms with short stems are attractively displayed against the bright dark green of the leaves. This bush tends to be wider than tall, making it useful for low hedging or borders. The overall appearance is very decorative.

Hollandica
7′ x 7′
R. rugosa x 'Manetti' (Noisette hybrid) ?
Spek, The Netherlands, 1888

Frequently used as an understock (particularly for rose standards), but rarely grown deliberately as a garden subject. Nevertheless, it is common to find 'Hollandica' whenever its budded stock has died back to the union. 'Hollandica' is thought to be a selection of *R. rugosa* or, perhaps, a hybrid with a noisette. Except for its more lanky growth, 'Hollandica' resembles *R. rugosa*. I question the noisette connection: this rose is exceedingly hardy and tenacious. 'Hollandica' is useful as a hedge rose because it is tall and suckers readily.

Hunter
4′ x 3′
R. rugosa **'Rubra'** x 'Independence' (Floribunda)
Mattock, England, 1961

I wish I could be more positive about this shrub but I've had two plants that did less than thrive, albeit the garden locations were less than ideal. While this rose does show promise, 'Hunter' does

HUNTER

not seem to have a strong constitution. I will try again, this time providing better conditions.

The bright red double blossoms are mid-sized, recurrent, and fragrant. The dark green glossy foliage is in scale with the flowers. Grown under ideal conditions this should be a most appealing, bushy shrub. 'Hunter' is reputedly very hardy but again I might question this claim since a floribunda is in its heritage.

Iwara (**R.** x *iwara*)

R. *multiflora* x **R. rugosa**
Japan before 1830

A curious, naturally occurring species cross having clusters of small white single flowers with separated petals giving the blossoms a blackberry-like appearance. 'Iwara' is non-recurrent and does not set hips. Its name means "rose thorn" in Japanese.

R. x *jacksonii* (See 'Lady Duncan'.)

Jens Munk
5′ x 5′
'Schneezwerg' x 'Fru Dagmar Hastrup'
Canadian Explorer Series, Canada, 1974

The blossoms are clear bright mid-pink. The semi-double flowers consist of approximately 25 petals and measure 2½ to 2¾ inches across. The inner petals frequently twist and sometimes partially obscure the center of gold stamens; often the petals have a white streak. There is a fresh spicy fragrance. The foliage is dense mid-green and somewhat small for a rugosa. This variety is vigorous and quickly establishes a particularly attractive, well-rounded form. 'Jens Munk' sets hips but they are sparse. As part of the Canadian Explorer Series this rose is, as one might expect, very hardy. One of my favorites, 'Jens Munk' exhibits a balance of excellent form, quality foliage, and attractive blossoms.

Kamtchatica (**R.** x *kamtchatica*)
7′ x 6′
R. *davurica* x **R. rugosa**
Kamtchatka (Russia), circa 1770

Probably a wild species hybrid, this rose was found in Russia. The lightly scented single blossoms are smaller than those of *R. rugosa* and are deep bright pink. The foliage bears a resemblance to the rugosas yet the canes are thinner and less thorny. The small hips are plentiful, round, and bright red. 'Kamtchatica' is frequently listed as a rugosa but pure rugosa it is not.

Jens Munk

LADY CURZON

Lady Curzon

4' x 6'

R. macrantha x **R. rugosa 'Rubra'**

Turner, England, 1901

This is an inspired cross between two species. *R. macrantha*, endowed with a refined yet simple beauty, is one of the few species that makes a true-to-form climbing rose. In combination with *R. rugosa*, the resulting characteristics create an especially beautiful rose. The single flowers are clear light pink with the delicate crinkled quality of an Iceland poppy (*Papaver nudicaule*). The petals pale to almost white around the yellow stamens. This rugosa hybrid does not repeat its blossoms. But the fleeting beauty of its fragrant flowers are more cherished for this characteristic. The foliage is mid-sized, somewhat elongated, and a deep olive-green. New growth is lighter in color with reddish tinges. 'Lady Curzon' is luxuriant and procumbent, forming a large particularly vigorous shrub with more width than height. Even though this rose does not rebloom, the foliage and form are attractive enough to earn it a place in any rose garden where its size can be accommodated.

Lady Duncan

2' x 6'

R. wichuraiana x **R. rugosa**

Dawson, USA, 1900

Similar in appearance to 'Max Graf', and understandably so. 'Lady Duncan', a hybrid created before 'Max Graf', has the same parentage but with a reversal of seed and pollen parents. Three-inch, single, bright clear pink blooms with yellow stamens. 'Lady Duncan' blooms but once a season, has a trailing growth habit, and displays glossy foliage.

The botanical name, *R. x jacksonii* designates the species cross of *R. rugosa* x *R. wichuraina*. These hybrids, typified by 'Lady Duncan', have been in cultivation since the turn of the century.

Le Cid

'Conrad Ferdinand Meyer' x **'Belle Poitevine'**

Vigneron, Country unknown, 1909

Modern Roses 9 and the *Combined Rose List* are my main sources of information for this rugosa hybrid. Available in Switzerland, this rose is described as a vigorous large plant with bright crimson blossoms and very few hips.

Linda Campbell

5' x 8'

'Anytime' (Miniature) x **'Rugosa Magnifica'**

Moore, USA, 1991

Deep bright crimson three-inch blossoms borne in large clusters. Consistent repeat, upright growth and healthy disease-resistant foliage.

Mme. Georges Bruant

5′ x 4′

R. rugosa x 'Sombreuil' (Climbing Tea)
Bruant, France, 1887

The climbing tea lineage may account for this rose's negative tendencies: winter dieback in colder climates and somewhat lanky growth. That aside, this a lovely white rugosa. The blossoms, composed of large, wavy petals, are semi-double in form, recurrent, and sweetly fragrant. But my favorite aspect of this rose is the color of the foliage. 'Mme. Georges Bruant' displays tinges of rusty red in the growth tips and clusters of long, elegant buds. These complement the olive-green of the foliage. 'Mme. Georges Bruant' was considered by some to be the first truly worthy European rugosa hybrid.

Mme. Julien Potin

4′ x 4′

R. rugosa x 'Gloire de Dijon' (Climbing Tea)
Gravereaux, France, 1913

Introduced by the French firm of Cochet-Cochet, which claimed such famous roses as 'Blanc Double de Coubert', this rose has not fared as well as the firm's other crosses. Today it is infrequently listed in nursery catalogs. 'Mme. Julien Potin' bears large double flesh-pink blossoms. The color is obviously influenced by its tea rose parent. Vigorous growth and recurrent bloom, but exhibits a tendency toward mildew.

MARIE BUGNET

Marie Bugnet

3′ x 3′

('Thérèse Bugnet' x unnamed seedling)
x 'F. J. Grootendorst'
Bugnet, Canada, 1963

Pure white, double blossoms with good fragrance. After the early blooming species roses, 'Marie Bugnet' is one of the first to bloom in my garden. Bloom repeats throughout the season and continues into the fall. The leaves are elongated and folded suggesting a species rose in its heritage. The olive-green leaves with reddish stems and light green new growth combine to make this shrub's foliage unique. 'Marie Bugnet' does not form hips and the blossoms tend to be easily damaged by rain.

Martin Frobisher

5′ x 4′

'Schneezwerg' x ?
Canadian Explorer Series, Canada, 1968

A dense pillar-shaped rose with erect canes. The blossoms are the color of strawberries and cream with not the slightest hint of lavender. About 2½ inches across with a light, fresh fragrance and borne consistently throughout the summer. Especially non-rugosa, the smooth canes have few thorns and turn dark red in the winter. The healthy foliage is soft gray-green and somewhat small with new growth showing tints of olive and yellow-green. 'Martin Frobisher' does not set hips. This shrub is another par-

MARTIN FROBISHER

ticular favorite of mine and my only criticism it is that the spent blossoms don't drop quickly enough, particularly in wet weather.

Mary Manners
4′ x 3′
Sport of **'Sarah Van Fleet'** (?)
Leicester Rose Co., England, 1970

Closely resembling and most likely a sport of the hybrid rugosa, 'Sarah Van Fleet', the flowers of 'Mary Manners' are pure white instead of pink. The blossoms are semi-double to double and fragrant. With handsome, large, dark green leaves and a bushy upright form, 'Mary Manners' repeats throughout summer. Both this rose and its parent are slightly prone to rust.

Max Graf
2′ x 8′
R. rugosa x R. wichuraiana
Bowditch, USA, 1919

Some of the best and most inspired crosses are the simplest. 'Max Graf', a species hybrid, is an excellent rose. As a parent of the extensively bred R. kordesii, 'Max Graf' holds an important place in modern rose history. (See R. kordesii.)

The groundcover growth habit derived from R. wichuraiana is the most significant aspect of 'Max Graf'. This rose roots freely along its prostrate canes to form a dense and effective ground cover. 'Max Graf' is a successful ground cover not in the same sense as pachysandra is used but as an exciting way to add color and form to a slope. The foliage is dark green, glossy, and very healthy in appearance. The single, clear pink blossoms pale to near white at the center. Non-recurrent; however, blossoms are produced over a long period. Wichuraiana influence is also evident in the apple-like fragrance of the blossoms.

Röte Max Graf. Kordes, 1983. A R. kordesii x seedling hybrid with single medium red flowers.

Weisse Max Graf. Kordes, 1983. A seedling x R. wichuraiana hybrid with semi-double white flowers.

Both of the above are said to have been genetically built along the same lines as the original 'Max Graf'. It is claimed that the red and white versions resemble 'Max Graf' in growth habit. Yet these varieties exhibit less rugosa influence.

An unfortunate modern trend in rose nomenclature is to name a new rose after a successful rose in an attempt to ride

Max Graf

the popularity coattails of the namesake. By naming roses in this fashion, the hybridizer implies similarity of appearance and performance while, in fact, the newly named roses may have distinctly different breeding.

Micrugosa (*R.* x *micrugosa*)
5′ x 4′
R. roxburghii x **R. rugosa**
Before 1905

In cultivation before 1905 and discovered as a volunteer plant at the Strasbourg Botanical Institute. The blossoms of this species hybrid are large, single, and pale pink resembling those of its *R. roxburghii* parent, although the crinkled elongated foliage shows rugosa influence. *R.* x *micrugosa* is dense in growth and has rounded orange hips.

Micrugosa Alba (*R.* x *micrugosa* 'Alba')
5′ x 4′
R. roxburghii x **R. rugosa**
Hurst, England, 1910

The white form of *R.* x *micrugosa*. Slightly more fragrant and with paler green leaves. Both this rose and *R.* x *micrugosa* are recurrent and are useful as hedge roses.

Mrs. Anthony Waterer
4′ x 5′
R. rugosa x 'Général Jacqueminot' (Hybrid Perpetual)
Waterer, England, 1898

The same cross as 'Arnold' but this time producing a loosely double, deep crimson-red blossom with a strong fragrance. There is some rugosa influence in the foliage but both the foliage and flowers lean more toward the hybrid perpetual parent. The growth is vigorous and the leaves are an attractive matte dark green. 'Mrs. Anthony Waterer' has some rebloom.

MRS. ANTONY WATERER

Mrs. John McNab

Mrs. John McNab

5′ x 5′

R. beggeriana x **R. rugosa**

Skinner, Canada, 1941

Rarely used by hybridizers, *R. beggeriana* demonstrates its influence in the foliage and late bloom of this rose. The fragrant blossoms of 'Mrs. John McNab' are the palest blush pink, semi-double and flat with a prominent center of yellow stamens. The form of the blossoms is similar to that of 'Schneezwerg' or 'Henry Hudson'. The growth is somewhat arching and open but still pleasing and graceful. Bright green matte foliage, sparse thorns, and reddish canes further enhance its appeal. 'Mrs. John McNab' is non-recurrent.

Two interesting asides about 'Mrs. John McNab'. First, this rose is frequently listed under a misspelled name, 'Mrs. John McNabb'. Dr. Skinner correctly spells the name of his own rose throughout his book, *Horticultural Horizons*. Second, there once was a 'Mr. John McNab', a rose with deeper pink flowers whose breeding included 'Kamtchatica'. 'Mrs. John McNab' remains available; 'Mr. John McNab' (Skinner, 1938) seems to have vanished from commerce.

MOJE HAMMARBERG

Moje Hammarberg

4′ x 4′

Parentage unknown

Hammarberg, Sweden, 1931

Lovely, large, asymmetrical, and loosely double blooms. The flowers could be compared to those of 'Rugosa Magnifica' except that they have more substance and are a more purple shade of crimson-purple. The yellow stamens are well displayed against the deep tones of the blossom. This rose has a strong rich fragrance, repeat flowers, and scarlet hips. The dark green foliage is large and of obvious rugosa disposition. The shrub is well formed, densely foliated, and very hardy. 'Moje Hammarberg' is not widely available but merits more attention.

Nigel Hawthorne

Hulthemia persica x **Rosa 'Harvest Home'**

Harkness, England, 1989

Pointed buds open to single blossoms of light salmon-pink with deep scarlet at the base of the petals. The flowers are slightly cupped, pale as they age, and have a light spicy fragrance. The foliage is mid-sized and somewhat glossy. Sparsely produced small green hips. Growth is low and spreading.

An intergeneric hybrid, x 'Nigel Hawthorne' is a milestone in rose breeding. *Hulthemia persica* very closely resembles a rose and was formerly classified as a subgenus of *Rosa*.

Nova Zembla
6′ x 5′
Sport of **'Conrad Ferdinand Meyer'**
Mees, England, 1907

'Nova Zembla' is a blush white sport of 'Conrad Ferdinand Meyer' and in every aspect except color resembles its parent. Both 'Conrad Ferdinand Meyer' and 'Nova Zembla' have wonderfully colorful new canes. The straight strong canes are well armed with thorns and when back-lit by the sun are a deep bright red providing a pronounced element of color in the garden. I find the canes of these two roses quite prone to winter damage in Maine's harsh climate. But given the extreme vigor of these roses, this is perhaps an advantage since it keeps them within reasonable bounds.

NOVA ZEMBLA

PAULII

Nyveldt's White
5' x 4'
(**R. rugosa** 'Rubra' x *R. majalis*) x *R. nitida*
Nyveldt, Holland, 1955

Although a hybrid, this rose resembles *R. rugosa* 'Alba' except for more arching growth and lighter green leaves. The single pure white flowers are large (4 inches across) and borne in clusters. Other attributes are recurrent blossoming and good fragrance. Dense but thorny growth make 'Nyveldt's White' suitable for hedging. Regretfully this rose, created with the lineage of a Western Hemisphere rose (*R. nitida*), seems to be available only in Europe.

Paulii (**R.** x *paulii*)
3' x 8'
R. arvensis x **R. rugosa**
Paul, England, prior to 1903

Despite its thorniness, vigor, and stout canes, *R. paulii* is a rose of unusual and delicate beauty. The snow-white petals are nar-

41

row and widely separated, resembling a clematis. The flowers are scattered over the dark rugosa foliage like fragrant stars. The beauty is fleeting since *R. paulii* does not rebloom, which is unusual for a rugosa hybrid but perhaps fitting for this rose. A dense low-growing habit makes this rose an effective ground cover and, because its canes are well-armored with thorns, it can also serve as a formidable low hedge. *R. x paulii* is sometimes sold under the older designation *R. rugosa repens alba*.

   ***R. x paulii* 'Rosea'** (*R. rugosa repens rosea*) is similar to the white form but has wider, pale pink petals and is less vigorous. Both bear a good crop of attractive hips.

Pavement Series
3′ x 3′
Hybrid rugosas. Parentage (?)
Hybridizer (?), Germany, Date unknown

Introduced into U.S. commerce in 1988–89, these are compact low-growing typically rugose shrubs. Dense healthy foliage, good disease resistance, and very hardy. All three roses are semi-double with centers of gold stamens. They are fragrant, repeat, and bear red hips.

Pirette Pavement. Light pink.
Purple Pavement. Purple-crimson not unlike 'Rugosa Magnifica'.
Snow Pavement. White with a hint of lavender.

Pink Grootendorst (See 'F. J. Grootendorst'.)

Pirette Pavement (See "Pavement series.")

Prairie Maid
4′ x 4′
['Ophelia' (Hybrid Tea) x **Türke's Rugosa Sämling**]
x *R. spinosissima* var. *altaica*
Morden Experimental Farm, Canada, 1959

Double cream-colored blossoms with sweet fresh spinosissima fragrance. Late-blooming with some repeat. Compact growth with attractive foliage.

Purple Pavement (See "Pavement series.")

Rheinaupark
4′ x 4′
['Grüss an Bayern' (Floribunda) x unknown seedling]
x *R. rugosa* seedling
Kordes, Germany, 1983

Some resemblance to 'Robusta' but with larger (about 4½-inch) and fuller blossoms of the same vivid scarlet-red. Good repeat bloom and a light fragrance. The growth is vigorous, full, and upright with large glossy dark green foliage.

Robusta
5′ x 4′
'Regeliana' (Rugosa) x unnamed seedling
Kordes, Germany, 1979

This is a bright flaming scarlet rugosa hybrid that still looks and behaves like a rugosa. Deep but brilliant red single blossoms

Robusta

with large wavy petals and a light fragrance. Angular growth and large, shiny deep green foliage showing definite rugosa tendencies. The dark foliage and intense red flowers make quite a dazzling combination. Good repeat bloom and vigorous robust appearance of this shrub make 'Robusta' a superior choice where a red rugosa is needed. 'Robusta' does have an affinity for blackspot but because of its vigor it seems to outgrow this affliction as the summer progresses.

I was unable to find an adequate description of the parent, 'Regeliana' except that it is said to be a rugosa variety.

Rose à Parfum de l'Haÿ

4′ x 4′

[*R. x damascena* x 'Général Jacqueminot'
(Hybrid Perpetual)] x ***R. rugosa***
Gravereaux, France, 1901

Although less rugose in appearance than other rugosa hybrids, 'Rose à Parfum de l'Haÿ' still exhibits rugosa characteristics. Large semi-double cherry-red blossoms with lilac overtones. Strongly fragrant, as the name implies, and recurrent but does not set hips. The foliage is deep green and somewhat modern in appearance but dense in growth. It is unfortunate that 'Roseraie de l'Haÿ' and 'Rose à Parfum de l'Haÿ' have names so similar because although quite different these two are often confused and mislabeled. This may also account for the different descriptions of this rose.

Roseraie de l'Haÿ

6′ x 5′

Sport or hybrid of *R. rugosa* 'Rosea'? Disputed.
Cochet-Cochet, France, 1901

Large semi-double to double blossoms of a deep intense purple-crimson hue with visible cream-colored stamens. A strong rich fragrance and particularly beautiful long scrolled buds. 'Roseraie de l'Haÿ' repeats well but sets few hips. The dark and luxurious leaves are a superior example of *R. rugosa* foliage. The form is dense and somewhat wider than tall. This is a lovely rose and deserves to be named after one of the most famous rose gardens in the world.

Röte Max Graf (See 'Max Graf'.)

Rugelda

5′ x 4′

Parentage unknown
Kordes, Germany, 1989

Fragrant lemon-yellow semi-double blossoms brushed with crimson. With its long-flowering and vigorous growth habit, 'Rugelda' resembles the rugosas. This rugosa hybrid is reasonably hardy: winter dieback may occur in colder regions.

Rose à Parfum de l'Haÿ

45

Roseraie de l'Haÿ

46

RUGOSA MAGNIFICA

Rugosa Magnifica

4' x 5'

Parentage unknown

Van Fleet, USA, 1905

The large 3½-inch blossoms are very similar in form and color to those of 'Hansa' but the blossoms of 'Rugosa Magnifica' are slightly less double with a more open appearance. Also, the light yellow stamens are more visible. The flowers have a spicy fragrance and are usually formed in large clusters with dependable repeat bloom. Large, dark glossy green foliage. Spreading wider than tall, the growth of 'Rugosa Magnifica' is dense. Large showy orange hips in the fall. This rose should not be confused with the R. *eglanteria* hybrid 'Magnifica'.

R. x rugotida

3' x 4'

R. *nitida* x **R. rugosa**

Darthuis Nursery, Holland, 1950

A R. *rugosa* x R. *nitida* hybrid that favors R. *nitida*, a native American species. Single pink blossoms, shiny elongated foliage, and spreading form. Does not set hips. Extremely hardy (zone 2).

Rugspin

Parentage unknown
Denmark

This is a hybrid rugosa bred in Denmark but to date not easily obtained in the U.S. If I could find a source closer than an Australian nursery I would be tempted to order this rose for its deep wine-crimson coloring. The flowers are large, single, and fragrant; the foliage, typically rugose. 'Rugspin' bears attractive hips. Details of parentage and size have not been published; however, a brief description and photograph appear in Trevor Griffiths' *Book of Old Roses*.

Ruskin

4' x 5'
'Souvenir de Pièrre Leperdrieux' x 'Victor Hugo'
(Hybrid Perpetual)
Van Fleet, USA, 1928

Any rugosa tendencies inherited from the seed parent are not evident in the strongly fragrant, double, crimson-red blossoms. In contrast, the large, attractive, mid-green foliage shows definite influence, as do the thorny canes. In colder climates, the blossoms are lovely but few in number. Wet weather can damage the blossoms. Perhaps in more moderate regions, 'Ruskin' might be a worthwhile rose. Repeat bloom.

Sarah Van Fleet

5' x 4'
R. rugosa x 'My Maryland' (Hybrid Tea) ?
Van Fleet, USA, 1926

The clear mid-pink blossoms are quite large, 3½ inches across, somewhat cupped, and semi-double. Although unlike that of rugosas, the fragrance of 'Sarah Van Fleet' resembles the scent of old garden roses. This shrub is a reliable bloomer; blossoms abound into the fall. The growth is angular and erect, the foliage is dense, and the overall effect of the shrub is very pleasing. The large handsome leaves are elongated and glossy bright green; the foliage is always attractive. Further enhanced by its consistent bloom, 'Sarah Van Fleet' is a good shrub for a mixed rose garden. The only negative: no hips. *Modern Roses 9* questions the pollen parent because of chromosome number.

Sarah Van Fleet

Scabrosa

6′ x 4′

R. rugosa seedling

Introduced by Harkness & Co., England, 1950

A chance seedling of unknown background but in essence a delightful and exaggerated version of the species rugosa. So often, contrary to the direction taken by some plant breeders, bigger is not better. But in the example of 'Scabrosa' very few would deny that this rose is an improvement upon the species. Almost every aspect of this shrub is larger: the blossoms, the foliage, the hips—all without losing any refinement. Very large, deep crimson-pink blossoms; dark, robust, healthy foliage; crab apple-size hips; strong, dense, vigorous growth. 'Scabrosa' also boasts a heavy fragrance and consistent rebloom throughout the summer. An excellent shrub with more than enough character and refinement to be an asset in any garden.

Schneelicht

6′ x 6′

R. rugosa x R. phoenicia

Geschwind, Hungary, 1894

It is curious that although R. phoenicia, the recorded pollen parent, is a tender and slender-caned climber with few thorns, its progeny 'Schneelicht' is a very hardy, very thorny, and dense-growing shrub. Clusters of blush pink buds open to large, fragrant, single, snow-white blossoms. The flowers are borne along the canes and the shrub develops into a well-rounded mound. General growth characteristics lean toward those of the rugosa parent. The once-flowering trait is inherited from R. phoenicia. 'Schneelicht' with its vigorous dense thorny growth is a good choice for hedging.

Schneezwerg

4′ x 4′

R. rugosa x R. bracteata

Lambert, Germany, 1912

A dispute surrounds whether or not the pollen parent of this shrub is R. bracteata. I have listed this parentage because 'Schneezwerg' indeed bears a marked resemblance to R. bracteata. The blossoms are snow-white, semi-double, and mid-sized, opening flat to display a handsome center of creamy stamens. The blooms are fragrant and repeat consistently throughout the summer. The small, deep forest-green foliage is glossy and dense. Numerous small, bright scarlet hips are effectively displayed against the foliage. My only criticism of this

SCHNEEZWERG

51

delightful rose is that it has, for me, been slow to establish. On the other hand, it is well worth the wait. Although *R. bracteata* is somewhat tender, 'Schneezwerg' is very hardy. ('Schneezwerg' is also listed as 'Snow Dwarf'.)

Signe Relander

6′ x 5′

R. rugosa hybrid x 'Orléans Rose' (Polyantha)
Poulsen, Denmark, 1928

In its fringed-flower form and in its growth habits, this rose resembles the Grootendorst roses; however, unlike the Grootendorsts, 'Signe Relander' offers fragrance. Small, double blossoms are borne in clusters. Bright deep red. 'Signe Relander' blooms freely and repeatedly.

Simonet's

6′ x 5′

R. macounii x **'Mme. Georges Bruant'**(?)
Simonet, Canada, Date unknown

The very double blossoms of this hybrid rugosa are mid-sized and pink. No repeat. Hardy.

Sir Thomas Lipton

6′ x 5′

R. rugosa **'Alba'** x 'Clotilde Soupert' (Polyantha)
Van Fleet, USA, 1900

Unfortunately, this poor representative of the rugosa hybrids is widely available. A number of large wholesale growers in the United States continue to propagate this rose despite its mediocrity. These growers are seemingly unaware that far better double white rugosa hybrids exist, such as 'Souvenir de Philémon Cochet'. 'Sir Thomas Lipton' is ungraceful and rigid in its growth and has the nastiest thorns imaginable. The first blossoms of the season can be appealing, but most are misshapen — especially the rare repeat blooms. The foliage is decidedly rugose but sparse.

Snow Pavement (See "Pavement series.")

Souvenir de Philémon Cochet

5′ x 4′

'Blanc Double de Coubert' sport
Cochet-Cochet, France, 1899

The very double flowers are large and pure white, sometimes with a hint of blush in the center. The appearance of the blossoms is somewhat unusual: large flat outer petals and densely packed inner petals mounding in the center resemble a double hollyhock. These blooms are not only beautiful but fragrant. Dependable repeat bloom. No hips. The foliage is handsome, deep rich green, and typically rugose. The dense vigorous

Souvenir de Philémon Cochet

Thérèse Bugnet

54

growth is restrained. I consider this rose to be distinctly different from its parent and much deserving of consideration in its own right.

Star Delight

2' x 2'

'Yellow Jewel' (Miniature Rose) x **'Rugosa Magnifica'**
Moore, USA, 1990

Low-growing, bushy habit. Single 1½-inch bright pink blossoms with a prominent white eye and a boss of gold stamens. The form of the blossoms resembles that of *R. x paulii*; the foliage exhibits rugosa influence.

Thérèse Bugnet

5' x 4'

[(*R. acicularis* x **'Kamtchatica'**)
x (*R. amblyotis* x *R. rugosa* 'Plena')]
x 'Betty Bland' (Hybrid Blanda)
Bugnet, Canada, 1950

THÉRÈSE BUGNET

This is clearly a complicated cross, one that is made even more so by 'Betty Bland' itself being a complex hybrid, *R. blanda* crossed with a hybrid perpetual. Not surprisingly, 'Thérèse Bugnet' is not particularly rugosa in character despite the genetic input of both 'Kamtchatica' and *R. rugosa* 'Plena'.

At first I thought this rose was overrated but must admit I've come to appreciate 'Thérèse Bugnet' more each year. The clusters of long, deep pink buds are very lovely. The large, dou- ble blossoms are mid-pink and very much "old rose" in charac- ter. 'Thérèse Bugnet' has a long first bloom period, some repeat during the summer, and additional bloom in the fall. The foliage is elongated, gray-green and disease resistant. The leaves, aug- mented by deep red canes, turn deep red in the autumn and are a pleasing sight. 'Thérèse Bugnet' is very hardy, experiencing little winter kill even in the most severe winters.

Thusnelda

6′ x 6′

***R. rugosa* 'Alba'** x 'Gloire de Dijon' (Climbing Tea)
Müller, Germany, 1886

Although both parents are recurrent, 'Thusnelda' blooms only once a season. The large semi-double blossoms are mid-pink and fragrant. Strong vigorous growth. An obscure rugosa hybrid. Only limited availability.

Topaz Jewel

5′ x 7′

Moore, USA, 1987

Yellow rugosas are always greeted with much fanfare as are new rugosa varieties sporting scarlet or other nontypically colored blooms. Rarely is the acclaim deserved. Despite my distrust, I purchased this rose and it has been a disappointment. Sometimes, although the various aspects of a rose may be individually pleasing, expectations are not met when the elements are combined. In my opinion, this occurs with 'Topaz Jewel', a rose whose modern name itself is unpleasant. Its semi-double pale yellow blossoms are rather nice, the growth is wide and angular; yet these features do not combine well. 'Topaz Jewel' is recurrent. It is prone to excessive winter damage in my harsh climate.

Vanguard

8′ x 6′

(*R. wichuraiana* x ***R. rugosa* 'Alba'**)
x 'Eldorado' (Hybrid Tea)
Stevens, USA, 1932

When I first ordered this advertised rose I was very excited by the prospect of a hybrid rugosa bearing large double blossoms of salmon color overlaid with golden tones; but that was before my gardening dreams of new colors were tempered by harsh reality. In this climate 'Vanguard' treads a fine line between barely hardy and not hardy. Sadly, all I've enjoyed from 'Vanguard' is the handsome large glossy foliage. Winterkill is excessive and if it weren't for this shrub's inherent vigor I wouldn't even see the foliage from year to year. In milder climates this shrub behaves vigorously, much like 'Dr. Eckener', and is said to have fragrant blossoms.

Wasagaming

6′ x 6′

(***R. rugosa*** x *R. acicularis*) x 'Grüss an Teplitz' (Bourbon)
Skinner, Canada, 1939

The pure simplicity of two species crossed with a bourbon of complicated ancestry (that includes a good portion of China rose) produces the delightful shrub 'Wasagaming'. The double mid-pink blossoms show hints of bourbon ancestry and limited aspects of its rugosa background. Good fragrance and recurrent bloom. I saw 'Wasagaming' in full bloom in mid-June in New Hampshire and was immediately taken with this rose. Its dense

TOPAZ JEWEL

rounded form was covered with lovely blossoms and it was a standout among hundreds of other roses in bloom. 'Wasagaming' is not difficult to propagate: this variety suckers readily. Oddly, it is not widely available.

Weisse Max Graf (See 'Max Graf'.)

White Grootendorst (See 'F. J. Grootendorst'.)

Will Alderman
4' x 4'
(**R. rugosa** x R. acicularis) x unknown Hybrid Tea
Skinner, Canada, 1954

Double lilac-pink blossoms with a center of gold stamens and a strong fragrance. The growth is dense and the form is rounded and bushy with good color in the canes for fall interest. Recurrent bloom. I don't know how I've missed this one but 'Will Alderman' is definitely on my "must have" list.

Yellow Fru Dagmar
4' x 4'
R. rugosa hybrid
France

This recent introduction offers fairly large, double blossoms similar to 'Agnes' in color. Foliage shows some rugosa influence. 'Yellow Fru Dagmar' is recurrent, does not set hips, and is of questionable hardiness for northern gardens. All and all, this rose is only remotely similar to its famous namesake. I could not find documentation of its parentage.

Cultivation

As an avid gardener who is open to experimentation, I hesitate to set down hard and fast rules for the culture of rugosas. Techniques I practice today could be contrary to those that I will use three or four years from now. Fortunately, rugosas are easy to please, surviving changes in cultivation methods and occasional outright mistakes. A garden grows and as it does so changes the gardener. Learning from experience dictates evolution. So, my first advisement is: take my advice with a grain of salt. Compare my practices to your own experiments and observe your plants' responses. Build and elaborate on the methods of cultivation that produce successful results in your garden with its unique demands.

The species, the natural forms 'Alba' and 'Rubra', and the simpler hybrids are the most adaptable rugosas. The most exceptional wild plants I've observed are those flourishing along the seashore where they have ample drainage, receive ocean moisture, and yet are in full exposure to the wind, sun, and salt. Rugosas clearly thrive with good air circulation and day-long sun; however, I have nice shrubs succeeding in a variety of contrary situations. Not only will rugosas grow in difficult sites such as along salted roadways or in oceanside plantings, they also prosper in hedge plantings, in naturalized areas where full sun is not always present, and in low-maintenance gardens. Functioning as shrubs, they bring to garden schemes the problem-solving benefits of repeat bloom, disease resistance, fall color, hips, fragrance, and naturally healthy foliage. If you have a difficult site and you want to place roses in it, the rugosas should be your first consideration.

Before you plant your newly acquired roses, know how they were propagated. Aside from 'Alba' and 'Rubra', which are sometimes sold as seedlings, or cutting-grown roses (therefore on their own roots), the majority of purchased rugosas are sold as two-year budded or grafted plants. Plant own-root roses at established soil lines. When planting a budded or grafted rose, I urge you to place the union one to three inches below soil level. This will encourage the rugosa to develop its own roots above the union. Deep planting usually eliminates suckering from the rootstock. Rootstock suckers, unwanted surprises, will not resemble the rose above the union and can wreck havoc with carefully planned garden schemes. Placing the union below the surface will also protect the plant from a harsh winter. If the canes should die back, the plant will not be lost to the rootstock. As many have preached before me: the size of the planting hole is critical. Dig a hole deep and wide so there is ample room to return loose, pliable soil around the roots. Whether you amend the soil before returning it depends on the soil type at your site.

Rugosas are erroneously thought to thrive only in sandy soils; but, I have large, well-established, impressive specimens growing in amended clay soil with less than ideal drainage. Clay from the planting hole is not returned. Instead, I prefer to plant rugosas with a half-and-half mixture of sand and very well-aged manure, old manure that has taken on the deep dark color and crumbly texture of compost. This mixture provides a rich and friable soil for quick root growth. I also mix a generous handful of bone meal or superphosphate into the bottom of the planting hole. While rugosas may take longer to reach potential in clay, the ultimate result is definitely satisfactory.

Rugosas purchased at a local nursery may be growing in containers. If purchased from a large nursery that has cold storage facilities or if purchased by mail order, the plants will have bare roots. Carefully remove roses from containers and plant without disturbing the soil around the tender roots. Check bare-root roses and remove any broken or damaged roots. Before planting bare-root roses, soak the roots overnight in a pail of water to which I recommend adding a dose of vitamin-hormone. (These natural compounds, that do not go against organic principles, are sold under various brand names.) When planting, set the rose firmly in the bottom of the hole and gently spread or fan its roots. (If the roots do not fit comfortably, enlarge the hole.) It is important to have the rose setting solidly in its new environment. Gradually add soil, tamping down each addition. Do not fill the hole completely; leave a concavity or hollow for watering around the newly planted rose. Water well in order to thoroughly soak the surrounding soil and eliminate air pockets.

I do not use chemical rose fertilizers on rugosas. My experience is that the chemical fertilizers are short-lived and promote leggy, uneven growth. Aged manure and bone meal (or superphosphate) are best for feeding. Do not use fresh manure. Horse manure is the substance of choice, but other types will do. (If bedding materials are present, be sure the manure mixture is properly aged – at least one year – to prevent nitrogen loss during decomposition.) To feed established plants, I apply two to four spadefuls of well-aged manure around each plant in the late fall, preferably after the ground has frozen or the plant has become dormant. This application will provide food for spring growth and it will also discourage mice and mole damage. I apply additional aged manure in the early spring to provide supplemental food and to serve as mulch.

Although many other roses depend on a rigorous program of chemical spraying, rugosas do not. Their robust foliage signals natural health. Spray a rugosa and its leaves will send a message well worth consideration: first the leaves will turn yellow, then brown before falling to the ground. Diseases and pests trouble rugosas less than other roses. Blackspot and mildew rarely bother the rugosas except some of the more complex hybrids. And rust is infrequent.

One unusually hot and humid summer, I was perplexed to see an incidence of canker on some of my rugosas. I pruned the infected canes well below the cankerous swelling and carefully disposed of them. The following summer there were very few cankers. I'd love to believe my diligent efforts were totally effective but acknowledge that the return of normal weather might also have been operative.

Few insects pester the rugosas and fewer still inflict lasting harm; however, Japanese beetles can cause damage. These pests, which thrive and breed in lawns or grassy areas, are likely to be rampant in your neighborhood if your garden is surrounded by a sea of mown grass. I attribute the absence of Japanese beetles in my own gardens to a prompt application of milky spore dust when I first heard local reports of these pests. The dust releases a naturally occurring disease that attacks Japanese beetle grubs. Very effective though not instantaneous, this organic control should be applied on a community-wide basis. The beetles will wander across boundaries to feast on your rugosas if your neighbors choose not to battle the beasts. Resilient rugosas will weather most onslaughts.

Without the use of sprays to combat diseases and pests, my reactions are simple, the remedies are blunt, and the treatment, direct. All organic solutions are applied. However, when a rose fails to respond, it is relegated to the garbage bin. Although some gardeners may disagree, I've had repeated disease problems with the Grootendorst roses and 'Sir Thomas Lipton'. Consequently those that were once in my gardens have long since departed via the waste disposal vehicle. Some wise person recently remarked that disposing of poor performers is the sign of an experienced gardener. This rings true. Many, many rugosas have strong constitutions—why waste time and space on poor performers?

Rugosas need not be pruned except to remove winter damage or deadwood in spring and to restrain or shape growth. I advise, particularly in harsh climates, against pruning during the fall or winter since this practice encourages additional dieback from the cut.

The rugosas need no winter protection: no rose cones, no burlap, no browning boughs. Enjoy the beauty of a winter garden without distractions. Rugosas with their strong thorny canes, definite character, and lingering hips are attractive winter specimens.

If you insist on perfect plants, you should strive to provide ideal conditions. But if your garden has demanding sites, remember rugosas do not need to be planted in sunny rose gardens, with perfect drainage and free-flowing air circulation. Use them to answer your design needs. Demanding little care, rugosas are year-round stars.

Rugosas in the Garden

S O MANY PLANTS TO TRY, so little time, so little space—plant selection and placement are not easy decisions for gardeners. I freely admit to being an obsessive and frequently impulsive gardener. I will never lay down my gardening gloves until I've grown everything that can possibly survive in my winter-ruled climate. And yes, as a result, little (and big) oddities are tucked away everywhere in the garden. Frequently doing little to complement the grand scheme, these whims are the asterisks of my garden. Rugosas are not whims, however. Instead, they function in a number of ways which directly enhance the overall planting scheme.

Vigor, hardiness, disease and pest resistance, varied blossom colors and forms, fragrance, rebloom, attractive foliage, fall color, hips, winter interest, and good growth form—all of the attributes of *Rosa rugosa* recommend this rose and its hybrids as plant selections worthy of a gardener's consideration. Desirable traits alone, however, do not more than an asterisk make! A superior garden plant must also attractively combine with its neighbors, ideally in a broad spectrum of possible utilizations and successful adaptations. The traits of rugosas, plus their tolerance of a wide range of garden conditions, allow design versatility.

Furthermore, rugosas function within garden schemes as more than ideal companions. Like trees, shrubs, and other larger plants, rugosas serve as framework plants or the structural bones in a garden design. Bones must be plants with good form and a long season of interest for they provide balance, maintain interest, and define the limits of a garden. Most garden roses would not meet these primary criteria; rugosas do.

Whether designing an overall landscape scheme (on whatever scale), a rose garden, or a border planting, the method of creating a harmonious plan follows one guiding consideration: thoughtful, problem-solving placement of structural plants. For example, when I design a rose garden the rugosa roses are usually placed first. Rugosas can be used to border the garden and to provide background and wind protection. Because they have good form and density I like to place rugosas throughout a rose bed to provide the substance required particularly late in the season when other surrounding roses may appear worn and leggy. In addition, rugosa roses' long season of bloom, including generally good-quality fall blossoms, contribute color and fragrance to the rose garden after many of the other roses have ceased to perform.

Moreover, when planning mixed beds or borders the structural considerations become critical. For maximum impact, a suitable background is needed to contrast and enhance the planting while the form and flow of the planting itself must be carefully orchestrated. Shrubs are frequently utilized in both of these design roles and again rugosas perform admirably.

Design challenges multiply as plans are made not for individual beds or borders but for entire landscape schemes; particularly problematic are those for newly constructed houses where no pre-existing plants are in place. The overall scheme must harmonize several individual areas: the ubiquitous foundation planting, paths and approaches to entrances or through the garden(s), borders and beds, and hedges. In each instance, rugosas are practical keys to solving these design problems.

Consider foundation plantings. Too frequently, this area is planted solely with evergreens. If you must have evergreens, interplant them with rugosas. Their blossoms, hips, and colorful fall foliage will interrupt the perpetual green of the evergreens. Rugosas are excellent in foundation plantings because they have the bulk and year-round interest necessary to meet the high-performance demands of this site. I offer only two caveats: do not plant under drip lines and beware of large eaves. An extended roof line will direct moisture away from the foundation and rugosas will not thrive in the resulting dry soil unless watered conscientiously. Plant beyond these dry-soil regions.

Along pathways, certain rugosas might be used as hedging. Thorny rugosa canes are a good deterrent to short cuts and keep traffic on the correct path. The Pavement series and 'Charles Albanel' are attractive possibilities. 'Fru Dagmar Hastrup' if pruned in the early spring can be restrained at a height of two and a half feet. A larger variety could be planted at pathway intersections to provide a point of interest. 'Martin Frobisher' functions well here. Its upright canes will not threaten to grab passers-by by falling outward into the pathway. If room permits 'Jens Munk' is a good choice, and if the path takes a sharp turn or has a V-shaped intersection, 'Souvenir de Philémon Cochet' will stop all visitors in their tracks with its beauty.

Rugosas make fine full-sized hedges. Cost-effective, they are generally less expensive and faster growing than other traditional hedging plants. Rugosa roses form a dense thorny barrier while providing a longer season of bloom than most other shrubs.

Single-variety hedges are less successful than mixed-variety hedges. This guidance comes from my observation that a gardener invites trouble if he or she plants symmetrically. Plants have no respect for symmetry. In fact, plants of the same variety, given the same growing conditions, will frequently grow at different rates. Should labor or chance produce symmetry, what happens if one or two plants die? Will you be able to find a source for the replacement? Will you be able to tolerate the asymmetry of a void? And so, if you want a rose hedge of uniform height, be forewarned.

An easier, less frustrating, and more aesthetically pleasing solution is to combine different varieties of similar heights. One combination would be to plant 'Thérèse Bugnet' toward the rear of the hedge because its smoky pink blooms tend to appear at the top of its growth. Build the hedge forward with dense-spreading varieties such as 'Rugosa Magnifica' and/or 'Blanc Double de Coubert'. These will quickly fill open pockets. To complete, use 'Belle Poitevine' with its soft pink blossoms playing against handsome dense foliage. The hedge will be a living tapestry of color and fragrance. Another option is to deliberately plant varieties of different heights. Choose lower varieties to reveal a pleasing view and taller ones to exclude eyesores in the landscape beyond the hedge.

There is a growing trend to use rugosa roses in commercial landscapes where low maintenance is a primary requirement. For the same reason, home gardeners will find rugosas to be valuable, attractive plants for wild or difficult sites. The varieties that sucker will form large clumps or mounds and could provide color in wild gardens or naturalized landscapes. The ground cover varieties such as 'Max Graf' are excellent on slopes or banking to hold the soil in place and prevent erosion. 'Lady Curzon' will prevent all traffic from attempting to pass through its dense growth. Reaching only three to four feet in height, its canes will snake and entwine to form an impenetrable ground cover. 'Mrs. John McNab', one of the quickest rugosas to establish, is a taller option for erosion control. A natural tolerance to salt makes rugosas useful in difficult sites near salted roads where little else will grow.

And lastly, if the above practical garden uses have not gained your appreciation for rugosas, I urge you to bring rugosas into your garden for the blossoms alone. The blossoms are very beautiful. The singles are enchanting in their pure simplicity and elegance of form. The doubles embrace all the richness and fascination inherent in the finest of old-fashioned roses. The colors and fragrances are inspirations to soothe the soul and lift the spirits. I have done justice to these lovely roses if I have at least coaxed you into trying one rugosa.

Historic Rugosas

RESEARCH reveals that current rose catalogs and plant source references do not include many of the interesting rugosa crosses that were developed in or before this century. Some modern varieties are even excluded. What has been the fate of the missing, the strayed rugosas? Despite the current lack of availablity, I decided to include the following rose descriptions, for these descriptions revive the visions of hybridizers from both sides of the Atlantic. Here are the exciting trials and errors, the crosses that utilize the strong genes of *R. rugosa*. Some of the roses in this section were never widely available. In France, for example, Gravereaux produced a substantial number of rugosa crosses, naming many varieties which were never introduced into commerce. Similarly, and sadly for northern gardeners, many of the Canadian rugosa crosses were never marketed.

Did poor disposition seal the fate of others? In a fascinating article that appeared in the 1917 *Journal of the International Garden Club*, H. R. Darlington recounts an era's efforts to meld the strong constitution of rugosas with the exotic coloration of early hybrid teas. Few gardeners would dispute that many hybrid teas lack longevity and resistance to disease. Did these new roses fail to inherit the healthy disposition of rugosas?

Surely not all the trials were failures. From published descriptions, seemingly ideal roses with unique worth were created. Some tenacious species crosses, and others such as the historically famous parent of the Kordes roses, exist in botanic gardens. Might others flourish, unnamed or incorrectly identified, in private rose gardens, backyards, or abandoned homesteads? Are any of these roses being offered by smaller local nurseries that do not market by mail order? Some undoubtedly are lost forever but others are surely extant.

I hope that this listing will be useful in several ways. The descriptions may help to identify obscure roses and those with deserving traits might be reintroduced into commerce. I hope readers will be inspired by these historic trials (and errors). Many possibilities are inherent in the genes of one of the hardiest of all roses, *Rosa rugosa*.

Agnes Emily Carmen
5' x 5'
R. rugosa x *R. x harisonii*
Carmen, USA, 1898

The hybridizer was probably hoping for a yellow rugosa (*R. x harisonii* is bright yellow), but instead created a double, bright crimson rose with profuse blossoms borne in clusters. Somewhat recurrent. The foliage is rugose.

Algonquin
10′ x 10′
Seedling of *R. rubrifolia* x unknown *R. rugosa* hybrid
Central Experimental Farm, Canada, 1928

Profuse large single rose-purple blossoms with white centers. The foliage is matte yellow-green. Large red bottle-shaped hips follow the blossoms. Vigorous, hardy, and non-recurrent.

Alysham
5′ x 5′
'Hansa' x *R. nitida*
Hansen (?)

Many large crimson double blossoms with light fragrance. Does not repeat. Dense, light green, glossy foliage.

Amdo
'Tetonkaha' x 'La Mélusine'
Hansen, USA, 1927

Large clusters of semi-double blossoms that are non-recurrent.

America
Parentage unknown
Introduced by Paul and Son, England, 1895

This is a rugosa hybrid sent from the Arnold Arboretum in 1892 to the nursery Paul & Son. The large purple-crimson blossoms are open in form and not particularly rugosa-like in character. Large spiny hips follow the flowers. This shrub blooms early in the season, an indication that 'America' possibly is a species hybrid. I can find no indication that this rose is still in commerce and, in fact, a modern climber has claimed its name.

Atropurpurea
5′ x 5′
R. rugosa x unknown *R.* x *damascena*
Paul & Son, England, 1899

Only limited information is available on this historic rose. Trevor Griffith's *The Book of Classic Old Roses* provides a brief description and a photograph. Although no current U.S. sources could be located, 'Atropurpurea' might be commercially available in New Zealand.

The name of this rose promotes confusion because *R. rugosa* 'Rubra' was formerly known as *R. rugosa* 'Atropurpurea'. Although both have single blossoms, this hybrid rugosa is quite different from the species form. Blackish crimson buds open into fragrant, deep crimson blooms that fade to purple. Also, the hybrid's blossoms are more open in form than those of 'Rubra'. Blossom petals are wavy. Round flattened hips. The foliage of 'Atropurpurea' exhibits both damask and rugosa influences.

Beauty's Blush
6′ x 6′
'Tetonkaha' x 'Pink Pearl' (Hybrid Tea)
University of Saskatchewan, Canada, 1955

Fragrant rose-pink double blossoms that pale with age. Vigorous and very hardy, 'Beauty's Blush' is without repeat bloom.

Benedikt Roezl
R. rugosa seedling x 'La France' (Hybrid Tea)
Berger, Germany, 1925

Pale carmine-rose flowers of good size. Dense rugose foliage. Vigorous growth habit. 'Benedikt Roezl' is recurrent.

Bergers Erfolg
R. rugosa seedling x 'Richmond' (Hybrid Tea)
Berger, Germany, 1925

Clusters of single 3½-inch blooms, crimson-scarlet with a light fragrance. Vigorous with dense dark foliage. Some repeat bloom.

Bernadette Chirac
R. rugosa x ['First Edition' (Floribunda) x 'Floradora' (Floribunda)]
Delbard and Chabert, France, 1979

Listed in *Modern Roses 9* as an apricot, yellow, and orange blend, this rose obviously favors the two floribundas in its parentage: 'First Edition', a coral-orange blend, and 'Floradora', an orange-red blend. Apparently not in commerce, and given my distrust of "curiosities," especially those of coloring, I would be surprised if this rose were anything to shout about. Rugosas are lovely; their blossoms need not be apricot or orange. In my opinion, these colors—unnatural to the species—are the commercially motivated products of modern rose breeding.

Betty Will
'George Will' x 'Betty Bland' (*R. blanda* hybrid)
Erskine, Canada, 1963

Double blossoms with vivid pink petals above, paler undersides. 'Betty Will' has long, arching red canes and dark green leathery foliage.

Bienyetu
4' x 7'
[Seedling from 'Pierre Notting' (Hybrid Perpetual) x 'Safrano' (Tea)] x **Conrad Ferdinand Meyer**
Gravereaux, France, 1906

This rose represents an early attempt to alter typical rugosa coloring. 'Safrano' is a tea rose of saffron and apricot; 'Pierre Notting', a dark red hybrid perpetual. The result, 'Bienyetu', is a double pink flower with touches of salmon; however, the quality of this flower's form is lacking. The growth habit of this shrub is broad and spreading. Attractive foliage. 'Bienyetu' does not appear to be in commerce.

Bonavista
'Schneezwerg' x 'Némésis' (China)
Svejda, Canada, 1977

Double, light pink, two-inch blooms freely borne. The flowers have a strong fragrance and are recurrent. Upright dense growth and light green foliage.

Caribou
'Ross Rambler' (Rambler) x (**R. rugosa** x *R. eglanteria*)
Central Experimental Farm, Canada, 1946

Large single white blossoms with a light fragrance but non-recurrent. The dark foliage, with the characteristic scent of *R. eglanteria*, is rugose. Dense and vigorous in habit and very hardy.

Carla
'Will Alderman' x **Hansa**
Erskine, Canada, 1963

Very similar to 'Hansa' but with more brightly colored flowers.

Carlsham
Hansa x *R. nitida*
Erskine, Canada, 1964

Large, deep pink, double blooms that repeat. Glossy foliage.

Chedane Guinoisseau

Parentage unknown

Guinoisseau, France, 1895

Fragrant double blossoms. Deep rose color. This shrub bears hips and is recurrent. Only briefly described in the *Journal of the International Garden Club*, this enigmatic rugosa may linger in old French gardens.

Cibles

R. rugosa '**Rubra**' x 'Perle de Lyon' (Tea)

Kaufmann, Germany, 1893

Scarlet blossoms with yellow centers. Vigorous upright growth.

Comte d'Épremesnil

7' x 7'

Parentage unknown

Nabonnand, France, 1892

H. R. Darlington, in his 1917 article on rugosas, described 'Comte d'Épremesnil' as a vigorous shrub with deep violet-crimson double blossoms. The parentage of this hybrid rugosa is obscure.

Conrad's Crimson

'Sweet Sultan' (Climbing Hybrid Tea)

x '**Conrad Ferdinand Meyer**'

Eacott, England, 1972

Fragrant three-inch double purple-crimson blooms opening flat. Light green foliage highlighted with touches of bronze.

Coppery Heart

'Peace' (Hybrid Tea) x '**Conrad Ferdinand Meyer**'

Gaujard, France, 1958

Recurrent blossoms in yellow-copper tones with touches of red. Dark glossy foliage and very vigorous growth.

Daniel Lessueur

['Pierre Notting' (Hybrid Perpetual) x 'Safrano' (Tea)]

x *R. rugosa*

Cochet-Cochet, France, 1908

From a different hybridizer, also seeking to create unusual coloring, this is a cross similar to that of 'Bienyetu'. Well-shaped large double yellow blossoms emerge from copper-tinged pink buds. Vigorous growth, straggling form, a profusion of hips. 'Daniel Lessueur' shares the fate of 'Bienyetu'; neither is in commerce today.

Daybreak

'Hansa' x *R. macounii* (*R. woodsii*) ?

Erskine, Canada, 1960

Deep pink double blooms. No additional descriptive information is available. Of interest primarily to rose breeders. 'Daybreak' was never introduced and was likely hybridized with the intent of using it in future breeding programs.

Dolly Varden

4' x 4'

R. rugosa hybrid of unknown parentage

Paul and Son, England, 1914

Pointed, deep apricot buds open to semi-double peach-pink blossoms with a yellow base. The foliage is modern in appearance and growth is vigorous. Recurrent.

Dorothy Fowler

3' x 3'

R. rugosa x *R. acicularis* x *R. spinosissima*

(Parentage not clearly recorded)

Skinner, Canada, 1938

Very fragrant, clear mid-pink 3½-inch blooms, semi-double and non-recurrent.

Dutch Hedge (See "Hedge series.")

Elle
'Schneezwerg' x 'Splendens' (Gallica?)
Lundstad, Norway, 1980

I suspect that the pollen parent of this rose is the gallica 'Splendens' not the white *R. avensis* hybrid 'Splendens'. 'Splendens' is the name used by some gardeners for the crimson *R. gallica* 'Officinalis' and considering that the blossoms of 'Elle' are semi-double, deep pink, very fragrant and non-recurrent, the gallica would seem to be the likelier parent. (There is also a gallica rose offered in several sources as 'Splendens'; its description is very similar to that of 'Officinalis'.) 'Schneezwerg' and the alleged avensis hybrid are both white, and it would be curious for two white roses to produce a deep pink descendent.

The growth is described as dense and vigorous. I'm sorry that this rose is difficult to obtain since the cross would prove quite interesting.

English Hedge (See "Hedge series.")

Erie Treasure
6′ x 6′
'Souvenir de Pièrre Leperdrieux' x **'Nova Zembla'**
Wedrick, Canada, Date unknown

Blush white double blossoms with a strong fragrance. Rugose foliage, vigorous growth and recurrent bloom.

Fern Kemp
'Conrad Ferdinand Meyer' x 'Frau Karl Druschki'
(Hybrid Perpetual)
Kemp, USA, Date unknown

Very fragrant, very large, semi-double, pale blush pink blossoms. Vigorous and hardy.

Georges Cain
'Souvenir de Pierre Notting' (Tea) x **R. rugosa**
Müller, Germany, 1909

A large, double, crimson-purple rose with a very vigorous growth habit.

Germanica
4′ x 4′
Parentage unknown
Müller, Germany, 1890

Introduced by Gravereaux, this rose is most notable in that it is one of the parents of 'Conrad Ferdinand Meyer'. 'Germanica' has single rose-pink blossoms. Little additional information is available. It seems to have disappeared from cultivation since 'Germanica' is not commercially available and I find few references to it.

Gneisenau
6′ x 6′
[**'Schneelicht'** x 'Killarney' (Hybrid Tea)]
x 'Crimson Rambler' (Rambler)
Lambert, Germany, 1924

Clusters of pure white non-recurrent double blossoms. This one appears to have been an attempt at producing a rugosa rambler. Was this cross successful?

Golden King
'Dr. Eckener' sport
Beckwith, England, 1935

Regarding 'Golden King' I can find little information and no sources. Although a sport of 'Dr. Eckener', it is apparently quite unlike its parent. The blossoms are loosely semi-double and pale yellow. It is recurrent and very fragrant. Being a sport of its parent, I can't imagine it would be a great improvement over 'Dr. Eckener' as a garden subject. Not reliably hardy.

Grace
5′ x 5′
R. rugosa x R. x harisonii
Saunders, Canada, 1923

Another yellow rugosa by the hybridizer who created 'Agnes'. Despite its similarities to the popular 'Agnes', 'Grace' has fallen from the lists of available roses.

Fragrant, very double blooms, pale amber with touches of apricot. As with 'Agnes', the foliage is very crinkled with a habit of dense growth. No repeat bloom occurs.

Hansette
'Hansa' x R. rubrifolia
Wright, Canada, 1938

A semi-double crimson hybrid without repeat bloom.

Hedge series
(R. rugosa 'Rubra' x R. majalis) x R. nitida
Nyveldt, Holland, Date unknown

The following roses all exhibit upright dense growth, ideally suited for hedging plants. (R. majalis, the Cinnamon Rose, is often listed under its older name, R. cinnamomea.)

Dutch Hedge. 1958. Small, single, pale pink flowers and red-orange hips.

English Hedge. 1959. Pink blossoms and red hips.

Pink Hedge. 1956. Pink blooms, bronzy foliage and red hips.

Red Hedge. 1958. Crimson flowers and scarlet hips.

Snow Hedge. 1963. White larger blooms and red hips.

Heidekind
'Mevrouw Nathalie Nypels' (Polyantha)
x unknown R. rugosa hybrid
Berger, Germany, 1931

Clusters of bright pink double blossoms with copper-crimson overtones and a light fragrance. Foliage somewhat rugose. This rose was patented and must have enjoyed some measure of popularity but is no longer in commerce. Another rose has claimed its name.

Hildenbrandseck
8′ x 5′
'Atropurpurea' x 'Frau Karl Druschki' (Hybrid Perpetual)
Lambert, Germany, 1909

Lambert, a German hybridizer, was also the originator of 'Frau Karl Druschki' (1901). The 'Frau' is an extraordinary rose in that it is still widely available and, in fact, I'm not sure that it has ever fallen from favor. In contrast, 'Hildenbrandseck' is no longer in commerce. 'Hildenbrandseck' blooms in clusters of single clear pink flowers. Vigorous growth and repeat bloom.

Julia Bugnet (See 'Lac La Nonne'.)

Kitana
'Tetonkaha' x 'Rose Apples'
Hansen, USA, 1927

Profuse bloom of semi-double deep lavender-pink flowers followed by red hips. Heavy fragrance. No repeat bloom.

R. x kochneana
R. carolina x R. rugosa

The growth habit of this species hybrid resembles its North American parent, R. carolina, but with larger, more intensely colored flowers of purplish red. Low-growing, slender thornless canes.

R. kordesii
'Max Graf' seedling
Kordes, Germany, 1950 (?)

Never marketed to the rose-growing public but, nevertheless, an undeniably important parent plant in rose history. *R. kordesii* was a spontaneous tetraploid seedling of 'Max Graf'; whether or not it is a hybrid is unclear. Various dates from 1940 through 1952 are cited. Kordes recognized and utilized its value in his breeding programs of vigorous and hardy climbing roses. The cupped, semi-double blossoms are deep pink and the foliage, glossy bright green. Its growth habit resembles that of its parent 'Max Graf'.

Koza
7 ′ x 6 ′
[*R. rugosa* seedling x 'La France' (Hybrid Tea)]
x **'La Mélusine'**
Hansen, USA, 1927

Semi-double deep pink. This rose has very vigorous and very hardy tendencies.

Lac La Nonne
7 ′ x 7 ′
R. rugosa 'Plena' x *R. acicularis*
Bugnet, Canada, 1930

Since Canadian rose breeders are concerned with hardiness, it is not surprising to see *R. acicularis* (zone 2) appearing in their crosses. 'Lac La Nonne' is extremely hardy. The three-inch flowers are semi-double and deep crimson-pink. Deeper crimson buds. Blossoms are medium-sized and fragrant. The growth is vigorous. Blooms late and does not repeat.

Julia Bugnet and **Nipsya Rose**. Bugnet. Canada. 1930. *R. rugosa* 'Plena' x *R. acicularis*

These roses have disappeared but it is interesting to note that they are the same cross as 'Lac La Nonne', created in the same year by the same hybridizer. Although 'Julia Bugnet' is named after a family member of its hybridizer, an honor that frequently denotes a rose possessing impressive qualities, this rose must have been dethroned by the superior 'Lac La Nonne'. I can find no descriptions of these roses other than in a listing of roses hybridized by Bugnet.

Lady Le-Ru
2½ ′ x 2½ ′
R. rugosa hybrid x unknown Hybrid Tea
Lothrup, USA, 1963

Large 3½-inch cupped double blossoms of deep pink with good perfume. The flowers are borne on long stems. Thornless canes. No repeat bloom. A small but hardy plant.

La Mélusine
Unknown *R. rugosa* hybrid
Spath, Germany, 1906

Clusters of large double blossoms, crimson-pink with a strong fragrance. Very vigorous growth. This lost German rose was significantly attractive to be extensively utilized in the breeding programs of the Canadian hybridizer Hansen.

Mme. Alvarez del Campo
Unknown *R. rugosa* hybrid
Gravereaux, France, 1906

Taller than wide, this rose is effective as a pillar rose and, safe to assume, vigorous. The breeding is unknown but could include the tea 'Safrano' since the blossoms are flesh pink with salmon tints—a combination that Gravereaux pursued.

Mme. Ancelot
8'–10' x ?
['Bourbon Queen' (Bourbon) x 'Maréchal Niel' (Noisette)]
x ['Perle des Jardins' (Climbing Tea) x **'Germanica'**]
Gravereaux, France, 1906

A bourbon cross noisette, crossed with a cross of a climbing tea and a rugosa, produced an unusually tall and somewhat ungainly hybrid rugosa. Not of particularly good quality, the large double blossoms are a pale flesh pink. Grown in New Zealand, 'Mme. Ancelot' is described by Trevor Griffiths in *The Book of Classic Old Roses*.

Mme. Ballu
Parentage unknown
Gravereaux, France, 1915

Rose-pink blossoms. Another Gravereaux hybrid that has fallen from the lists of available roses. Was its fate sealed by poor performance? The description of 'Mme. Ballu' in the *Journal of the International Garden Club* mentions inferior blossom form.

Mme. Charles Frederic Worth
6' x 6'
Unknown *R. rugosa* hybrid
Schwartz, France, 1890

Large clusters of double carmine blossoms and vigorous growth. Little information is recorded about this elusive rose yet I mention it because I find reference to it having been grown in Canada. 'Mme. Charles Frederic Worth' once held sufficient promise to be transported across the Atlantic and to attract the attention of rose breeders.

'Mme. Charles Frederic Worth' is cited in an article published circa 1930, "Breeding Roses for Canada," by J. W. Crow. The same article also lists other currently obscure rugosa hybrids: 'Agnes Emily Carmen', 'Comte d'Épremesnil', and 'Souvenir de Pièrre Leperdrieux'.

It is obvious that these hardy roses were better known in the first part of the twentieth century. Does 'Mme. Charles Frederic Worth' flourish today in Canadian gardens, or possibly continental gardens, awaiting discovery?

Mme. Henri Gravereaux
'Marie Zahn' (Hybrid Tea) x **'Conrad Ferdinand Meyer'**
Gravereaux, France, 1905

Large, creamy-white, loosely double blossoms with a touch of pink in the center. A shrub of vigorous growth. There was another 'Mme. Henri Gravereaux', a hybrid tea by Barbier, France, 1926.

Mme. Lucien Villeminot
'Conrad Ferdinand Meyer' x **'Belle Poitevine'**
Gravereaux, France, 1901

This soft salmon-pink rose in growth and form resembles its seed parent. Attractive large double blossoms not quite as full as 'Conrad Ferdinand Meyer'. Good repeat. Sadly, despite its superior lineage, this rose seems to no longer be in commerce.

Mme. Ph. Plantamor
1900

Semi-double deep crimson blossoms. Both blooms and foliage are reminiscent of those of 'Mrs. Anthony Waterer'. Photograph and description appear in Trevor Griffith's *A Celebration of Old Roses*.

Mme. Renee Gravereaux
'Conrad Ferdinand Meyer' x 'Safrano' (Tea)
Gravereaux, France, 1906

Again, a cross containing limited rugosa influence and, presumably, resulting in a less hardy rose. The double blossoms are cupped and soft pink.

Mme. Tiret

['Pierre Notting' (Hybrid Perpetual) x 'Cardinal Pattriyi' (Type unknown)] x **'Germanica'**

Gravereaux, France, 1907

It is unfortunate that so many of these Gravereaux roses have disappeared from commerce. This rose, in particular, sounds quite interesting. It is described in the 1917 *Journal of the International Garden Club* as being carmine with pale pink on the reverse of the petals. A vigorous shrub with attractive brown color in the canes. Recurrent?

Madeline Filot

['Queen of Bourbons' (Bourbon) x 'Perle des Jardins' (Climbing Tea)] x **'Germanica'**

Gravereaux, France, 1907

Did so many of these tender rose and rugosa crosses disappear because of fickle changes in taste or were the resulting roses truly inferior? Without having documentation of their failings, shouldn't we reinvestigate these past crosses? 'Madeline Filot' is a double rose-pink with deeper rose coloring on the reverse its the petals.

Martha Bugnet

6′ x 6′

(**'Kamtchatica'** x *R. amblyotis* x *R. rugosa* 'Plena')

x **'F. J. Grootendorst'**

Bugnet, Canada, 1959

Long, pointed buds open to large purple-crimson semi-double blossoms with a heavy fragrance. Dark rugose foliage and vigorous growth accompanied by repeat bloom. (Apparently, the hybridizer was not careful in recording details of the cross.)

Mary L. Evans

'Hansa' x *R. macounii*

Wright, Canada, 1936

Deep pink and non-recurrent. Very similar to 'Tetonkaha' but wider in growth.

Micmac

4′ x 4′

R. rubrifolia x unknown *R. rugosa* hybrid

Central Experimental Farm, Canada, Date unknown

Clusters of white bloom against deep purple-red foliage. Hardy with no repeat blossoming.

Minisa

R. rugosa x 'Prince Camille de Rohan' (Hybrid Perpetual)

Hansen, USA, 1927

Very fragrant deep crimson semi-double flowers with repeat bloom. Exceedingly hardy.

Mrs. MacDonald's Rose

R. rugosa 'Plena' x *R. acicularis*

Wright, Canada, Date unknown

Very similar to 'Lac La Nonne'.

Mohawk

R. rubrifolia x **R. rugosa**

Central Experimental Farm, Canada, Date unknown

Single blossoms described in *Modern Roses 8* as being "brighter than aster-purple" with a white eye. 'Mohawk' flowers profusely and the foliage is small, rounded, and matte green. This rose is hardy and does not repeat.

Moncton
'Schneezwerg' x *R. chinensis* cultivar
Svejda, Canada, 1977

The two-inch blossoms are profuse, light pink, double, very fragrant, and, surely, recurrent. The growth is upright and dense with gray-green foliage. Rugose or pointed? In researching rugosas, I found only two crosses utilizing *R. chinensis*: 'Calocarpa' and 'Moncton'. The former, which was introduced in 1895, remains available whereas the latter, which appeared in 1977, has apparently disappeared in less than two decades.

Moose Range
'Hansa' x **'Mary L. Evans'**
Wright, Canada, 1944

Almost identical to 'Hansa' but with sparse fall bloom.

Mossman
4′ x 4′
(*R. acicularis* x ***R. rugosa***) x unknown Moss rose
Skinner, Canada, 1954

Well-mossed buds and stems. 2½-inch pale pink, fully double blossoms of good form. A fascinating hybrid hopefully still extant and in cultivation. This hardy and unusual rose should hold commercial appeal.

Musician
'Hansa' x 'Hazeldean' (Hybrid Spinosissima)
Wright, Canada, 1953

Small clusters of semi-double blossoms. Grayish overtones partially dull the yellow-reds of 'Musician'. Somewhat rugose foliage, non-recurrent, and very hardy. This historic rose should be of interest to rose breeders since it was one of the first extremely hardy bi-color roses.

Nascapee
['Ross Rambler' (Rambler) x (***R. rugosa***
x *R. eglanteria*)] x (?)
Preston, Canada, 1946

Clusters of single white blossoms with a light fragrance. Very vigorous, good repeat bloom, and hardy.

New Century
4′ x 4′
***R. rugosa* 'Alba'** x 'Clotilde Soupert' (Polyantha)
Van Fleet, USA, 1900

Double, cupped, flesh-pink blossoms with darker centers and creamy edges. Some resemblance in form to the popular Van Fleet rose, 'Sarah Van Fleet'. Note the lack of resemblance between 'New Century' and 'Sir Thomas Lipton', a 1900 Van Fleet rose of identical breeding. The two could not be further apart in character, yet 'Sir Thomas Lipton' has survived, but the possibly superior 'New Century' has disappeared.

The recurrent blossoms of 'New Century' are fragrant. Growth is bushy and the foliage, light green.

Nipsya Rose (See 'Lac La Nonne'.)

Okaga
'Alika' (Gallica) x **'Tetonkaha'**
Hansen, USA, 1927

It is interesting that N. E. Hansen brought 'Alika' from Russia in 1906, probably with its breeding potential in mind. 'Okaga' is a semi-double deep pink. Very hardy with low dense growth. No repeat bloom.

Pink Hedge (See "Hedge series.")

Polyana
R. rugosa x a Polyantha
(possibly 'Mme. Norbert Levavasseur')
Skinner, Canada, 1923

In his book, *Horticultural Horizons*, Dr. F. L. Skinner describes raising an unnamed seedling rugosa in 1907, one which was identical to 'F. J. Grootendorst' but was apparently not hardy. 'Polyana' represents a second attempt by Dr. Skinner; yes, 'Polyana' is described as identical to 'F. J. Grootendorst'.

Prairie Charm
4′ x 4′
'Prairie Youth' (Shrub) x **'Prairie Wren'**
Morden Experimental Farm, Canada, 1959

Both parents of 'Prairie Charm' are complicated crosses involving some degree of rugosa parentage. 'Prairie Charm' produces semi-double salmon-coral blossoms. The foliage is light green, the growth is arching, and this rose is very hardy. Free-blooming but no repeat-flowering.

Prairie Sailor
6′ x 6′
Morden Experimental Farm, Canada, 1946

Another complicated cross, this time involving 'Türke's Rugosa Säm-ling', 'Dr. W. Van Fleet' (Large-flowered Climber), and *R. spinosissima* var. *altaica*. The single blossoms of 'Prairie Sailor' are deep yellow brushed with red. Profuse non-repeat bloom and reliable hardiness.

(*R. spinosissima* is considered by some *nomen ambiguum* and has recently been replaced by *R. pimpinellifolia*.)

Prairie Wren
6′ x 12′
Morden Experimental Farm, Canada, 1946

A combination of a hybrid tea ('Ophelia'), an unknown rugosa, and *R. spinosissima* var. *altaica*. Despite its hybrid tea parentage, 'Prairie Wren' is very hardy. Once-flowering. However, the lack of recurrent bloom is balanced by a copious display of large, rich pink, semi-double blossoms.

I cannot find a source for 'Praire Wren' or 'Prairie Sailor', but I would recommend that these roses be reinvestigated. Any rose resulting from the cross of *R. rugosa* with *R. spinosissima* var. *altaica* (a superlative hardy rose) should be worthwhile.

Prattigosa
3½′ x 3½′
R. prattii x **R. rugosa 'Alba'**
Kordes, Germany, 1953

Long pointed buds open to a profusion of large single pink blossoms. Lightly fragrant. Light green leathery foliage and vigorous upright growth.

Prof. N. E. Hansen
Unknown R. rugosa hybrid
Budd, USA, 1892

Little descriptive literature has survived on this rose – only its blossom coloration and name derivation. 'Prof. N. E. Hansen' has deep red blooms. This rose was named by an Iowa State professor after a South Dakota State College professor, one American rose breeder honoring another.

Proteiformis (*R. x proteiformis*)
***R. rugosa* 'Alba' x unknown diploid**

Introduced in 1894, this rose is a botanical "curiosity." The foliage is of interest because it varies from one end of the season to the other. At first, normal leaves appear. Later in the growing year, new growth becomes narrow, almost fern-like. It has been postulated that a virus condition causes the change. (Krüssmann, *Manual of Cultivated Broad-Leaved Trees and Shrubs*.) *R. x proteiformis* has clusters of white blossoms, semi-double. Occasional rebloom. Very little additional information is published on this unusual rose.

Quadroon
'Hansa' x ('Hansa' x *R. nitida*)
Wright, Canada, Date unknown

Poor growth habits. Single deep dark crimson blossoms and no repeat bloom.

Red Hedge (See "Hedge series.")

Regina Badet
['Général Jacqueminot' (Hybrid Perpetual) x 'Empereur du Maroc' (Hybrid Perpetual)] x ***R. rugosa***
Origin unknown

Very double, large, deep pink blossoms with a heavy fragrance. Dark foliage, bushy growth and recurrent bloom.

Rose Apples
5′ x 5′
Parentage unknown
Paul & Son, England, 1906

A little-known hybrid rugosa apparently no longer in commerce, if indeed it is still in cultivation. Large, semi-double, rose-pink, and fragrant blossoms. From the name 'Rose Apples', one could assume that the hips are large and prominent. This rose was imported by Hansen for rose breeding. (See 'Kitana'.)

Royal Robe
(*R. rugosa* x an unknown Hybrid Perpetual)
x (*R. multiflora* x *R. blanda*)
Wright, Canada, 1946

Large crimson-purple semi-double blossoms and vigorous growth. No repeat bloom.

Rugosa Copper
'Conrad Ferdinand Meyer' x unknown seedling
Gaujard, France, 1955

A large blossom in a copper shade of orange. Vigorous growth and recurrent bloom. 'Rugosa Copper' is elusive for a rose introduced as recently as 1955. As much of a novelty as this rose might appear to be, I can find no current suppliers. Perhaps other rose fanciers share my difficulty in envisioning an orange rugosa.

Sanguinaire
6½′ x 5′
'Bergers Erfolg' x 'Captain Ronald Clerk' (Hybrid Tea)
Gillot, France, 1933

Long pointed buds open to four-inch semi-double deep orange-red blooms with a boss of yellow stamens. 'Sanguinaire' has only a light fragrance and is recurrent. Glossy foliage.

Schwabenland
3′ x 3′
R. rugosa seedling x 'Elizabeth Cullen' (Hybrid Tea)
Berger, Germany, 1928

Profuse large blossoms of deep pink. Double, fragrant, and recurrent. Large deep green leathery foliage.

Sioux Beauty
'Tetonkaha' x 'American Beauty' (Hybrid Perpetual)
Hansen, USA, 1927

Fragrant, very double, bright rose-crimson blooms with a darker crimson center. 'Sioux Beauty' does not repeat and is hardy.

Smit's Briar
R. rugosa x R. canina
Smits, Holland, Date unknown

Once used as understock for budded roses, 'Smit's Briar' is a vigorous rose and most likely still survives in gardens where grafted or budded stock has died.

Snow Hedge (See "Hedge series.")

Souvenir de Christophe Cochet
6' x 6'
R. rugosa 'Alba' x 'Comte d'Épremesnil'
Cochet-Cochet, France, 1894

Large semi-double mid-pink blossoms with good fragrance. If this hybrid rugosa measures up to other Cochet-Cochet roses, then it is a shame that this rose is not available.

Souvenir de Pièrre Leperdrieux
4' x 4'
Parentage unknown
Cochet-Cochet, France, 1895

An early and now apparently lost hybrid most noted for its fragrance, a strong rose perfume with overtones of sweetbrier. Perhaps a hybrid of R. eglanteria? Large somewhat semi-double blossoms of a deep purple-carmine.

Souvenir de Yeddo
4' x 4'
R. rugosa x R. x damascena
1874

Fully double blossoms of clear mid-pink. The *Journal of the International Garden Club* attributes the parentage information to an 1893 article by Emilie Koehne in *Deutche Dendrologie*. Hybridizer not given. Color and doubleness of blossoms give credence to the influence of R. damascena.

R. x spaethiana
R. palustris x **R. rugosa**
1902

This species cross results in a hardy rose with carmine-pink blossoms, light green foliage, and abundant scarlet-red hips. Strong, upright growth habit. Krüssmann reports zone 4 hardiness. If this rose inherited its seed parent's tolerance for damp sites, it would be a very useful rose.

Stella Polaris
4' x 4'
Parentage unknown
Jensen, Germany?, 1890

Clusters of large double white flowers. Dark green fern-like foliage and vigorous growth habit. Repeat bloom.

Stern von Prag
R. rugosa seedling x 'Edward Mawley' (Hybrid Tea)
Berger, Germany, 1924

Large, deep red, double blossoms and large, dark green foliage. Dense vigorous growth, fragrant, and recurrent. Unfortunately, 'Stern von Prag' has not been listed in either European or American catalogs for decades.

The pollen parent, which has also lapsed into oblivion, was named after Edward Mawley who co-authored *Roses for English Gardens* with Gertrude Jekyll. No doubt a distinguished rose to bear the name of an established rosarian.

Symbole
'Mevrouw G. A. Van Rossem' (Hybrid Tea)
x **'Roseraie de l'Haÿ'**
Robichon, France, 1945

Very large well-formed carmine blooms with a light fragrance. The blossoms, displayed on long stems, are recurrent and free-blooming. Growth is vigorous.

Tegala
5' x 5'
'Tetonkaha' x 'Alika' (Gallica)
Hansen, USA, 1927

A non-repeat semi-double rose with deep pink blossoms. Very hardy.

Teton Beauty
'Tetonkaha' x 'American Beauty' (Hybrid Perpetual)
Hansen, USA, 1927

Very double cupped crimson-pink flowers. Recurrent and very hardy. 'Teton Beauty' has typically rugose foliage.

Tetonkaha
6' x 6'
R. macounii (R. woodsii?) x unknown *R. rugosa* hybrid
Hansen, USA, 1920

'Tetonkaha' offers one profuse bloom of deep pink mid-sized semi-double blossoms with a strong fragrance. A vigorous and hardy shrub, obviously of merit since it was used in so many of Hansen's crosses.

Therese Bauer
('Hansa' x *R. setigera*) x *R. setigera*
Ludwig (Introduced by Kem Nurseries), USA, 1963

Clusters of large semi-double mid-pink blossoms with a slight fragrance. Very vigorous, upright growth habit, and profuse repeat bloom. *R. setigera* is a lovely rose, tall-growing with blackberry-like foliage that should, when crossed with 'Hansa', produce a very attractive plant. (Interestingly, Krüssmann reports that in the mid 19th century *R. setigera* was widely used for hybridizing winter-hardy climbers.) 'Therese Bauer' is a rose that I would definitely want to grow.

Trollhättan
Little information is published on this rose. Trevor Griffiths provides a photo and a short caption in *The Book of Classic Old Roses* but does not mention breeding details, date or availability. Possibly available in New Zealand? 'Trollhättan' has mid-pink, loosely double blossoms that are similar in form to those of 'Rugosa Magnifica', but considerably lighter in color. Small, rugose leaves. The growth is described as mid-sized.

Türke's Rugosa Sämling
3' x 3'
'Conrad Ferdinand Meyer' x 'Mrs. Aaron Ward'
(Climbing Hybrid Tea)
Türke, Germany, 1923

Long pointed buds open to large semi-double yellow blossoms with peach and pink overtones. A strong fragrance. Dark leathery foliage, vigorous growth, and recurrent bloom.

Vira
Bohm, Czechoslovakia, 1936

Extremely fragrant, very bright red, and exceedingly vigorous. Details of this hybrid rugosa's parentage are not available.

Wadei (*R. x wadeii*)
R. rugosa x *R. moyesii*

A *R. rugosa* x *R. moyesii* curiosity with little to recommend it. Single pink flowers, yellow-green foliage and sprawling growth. Shepherd, in *History of the Rose*, describes the blossoms as salmon-pink, three inches across. Introduced in 1919.

Warleyensis (*R. x warleyensis*)
R. blanda x **R. rugosa**

A cross between *R. blanda*, a North American species, and *R. rugosa*, circa 1910. Single deep pink blossoms, thorny canes, and somewhat elongated foliage. *R. x warleyensis* sets half-inch red hips. An extremely hardy rose (zone 2) that has strayed.

Waskasoo
'Little Betty' (Hybrid Blanda) x **'Hansa'**
Erskine, Canada, 1963

Large, double, dark crimson flowers borne singly. Rugose foliage.

Wild Child
R. rugosa **'Rubra'** x 'Dortmund' seedling (Kordes Rose)
Hall, USA, 1982

A good dose of *R. rugosa* exists in the pedigree of this rose because the pollen parent of 'Wild Child' is a kordesii hybrid. The single, light pink blossoms have a tea fragrance, are borne in clusters, and are recurrent. Small leaves with rugose tendencies. The growth is somewhat arching and vigorous as its name implies. Why has this rose so suddenly dropped from sight? If a source could be located, I would immediately purchase 'Wild Child'. The name tempts me with its implications.

Yanka
'Tetonkaha' x ['Grüss an Teplitz' ? (Climbing Hybrid Tea)
x **'La Mélusine'**]
Hansen, USA, 1927

'Yanka' blooms in clusters of semi-double pink blossoms. Non-recurrent and extremely hardy.

Yatkan
'Grüss an Teplitz' ? (Climbing Hybrid Tea)
x **'La Mélusine'**
Hansen, USA, 1940

Double 2½-inch pink blossoms, non-recurrent, and very hardy.

Zika
[*R. rugosa* x 'Anna de Diesbach' (Hybrid Perpetual)]
x **'Tetonkaha'**
Hansen, USA, 1927

Fragrant semi-double pale shell-pink blossoms. Very hardy. 'Zika' is said to be non-recurrent which is questionable since two of its ancestors are repeat-blooming roses.

Table of Available Rugosas

NAME	SIZE	FOLIAGE	BLOSSOM COLOR	BLOSSOM SIZE	BLOSSOM TYPE	RECURRENT	FRAGRANT	HARDY	DISEASE RESISTANT	HIPS
ROSA RUGOSA	6 ft. x 6 ft.	Dark Green	Variable	Large	Single	Yes	Yes	Yes	Yes	Yes
R. RUGOSA 'ALBA'	6 x 6	Deep Green	White	Large	Single	Yes	Yes	Yes	Yes	Yes
R. RUGOSA 'RUBRA'	6 x 6	Dark Green	Deep Pink	Large	Single	Yes	Yes	Yes	Yes	Yes
AGNES	5 x 5	Lt. Green very crinkled	Amber Yellow	Medium	Double	No	Yes	Yes	Some	No
ALICE ALDRICH			Bright Pink	Large	Double	Yes				
AMÉLIE GRAVEREAUX	5 x 5	Dark Green	Purple-Crimson	Medium	Double	Yes	Very	Quite		
ANN ENDT		Small, Soft	Deep Crimson	Medium	Single		Yes	Yes		
ARNOLD	4 x 4	Dk. Green	Deep Pink	Large	Single	Yes	Yes	Quite	Yes	
BASYE'S PURPLE	3 x 3	Dk. Green	Dark Purple	Medium	Single	Yes	Yes	Yes	Yes	No
BELLE POITEVINE	5 x 5	Mid-Green	Soft Pink	Large	Semi-Dbl.	Yes	Yes	Yes	Yes	Some
BLANC DOUBLE DE COUBERT	5 x 4	Dk. Green Med. Size	White	Large	Double	Yes	Very	Yes	Yes	Yes
CALOCARPA	5 x 5	Elongated	Lilac Pink	Large	Single	No	Yes	Yes	Yes	Yes
CARMEN	4 x 4	Deep Green	Deep Crimson	Large	Single	Some	Yes			No
CARMENETTA	7 x 9	Glaucous	Pale Pink	Small	Single	No	Yes	Yes	Yes	
CHARLES ALBANEL	1 x 3	Light Green	Medium Red	Large	Double	Yes	Yes	Yes	Yes	
CONRAD FERDINAND MEYER	6 x 5	Large Dark Green	Medium Pink	Large	Double	Yes	Very	Quite	Some	No
CORYLUS	3 x 3	Sm. Elongated	Medium Pink		Single		Yes	Yes	Yes	Yes
CULVERBRAE	5 x 4	Vigorous	Crimson-Purple	Large	Double	Some	Very	Some		
DART'S DASH	4 x 4	Dk. Green	Purple-Crimson	Large	Sem-Dbl.	Yes	Yes	Yes	Yes	Yes
DART'S DEFENDER	4 x 4	Shiny	Violet-Pink	Medium	Single	No		Yes	Yes	
DAVID THOMPSON	4 x 4	Medium Green	Deep Pink	Medium	Double	Yes	Yes	Yes	Yes	No

Table of Available Rugosas (*continued*)

NAME	SIZE	FOLIAGE	BLOSSOM COLOR	BLOSSOM SIZE	BLOSSOM TYPE	RECURRENT	FRAGRANT	HARDY	DISEASE RESISTANT	HIPS
DELICATA	4 x 3	Dark Green	Lilac Pink	Large	Semi-Dbl.	Yes	Very	Yes	Yes	Yes
DR. ECKENER	8 x 6	Medium Green	Copper-Yellow	Medium	Double	Yes	Yes	Tender	Some	No
FIMBRIATA	4 x 4	Bright Green	Blush-White	Small	Double	Yes	Yes	Yes	Yes	Some
F.J. GROOTENDORST	5 x 4	Sm. Lt. Green	Crimson	Small	Double	Yes	No	Yes	Some	No
FLAMINGO	3 x 3	Gray Green	Deep Pink	Large	Single	Yes	Yes	Tender		
FRU DAGMAR HASTRUP	4 x 4	Dark Green	Pale Pink	Large	Single	Yes	Yes	Yes	Yes	Yes
GALLERIA	4 x 4	Medium Green	Silver Pink	Large	Semi-Dbl.	Yes	Very	Yes	Some	Yes
GEORGE WILL	4 x 4	Small	Lilac Pink	Large	Double	Yes	Yes	Yes	Yes	
GROOTENDORST SUPREME	5 x 4	Sm. Lt. Green	Deep Crimson	Small	Double	Yes	No	Yes	Some	No
HANSA	7 x 7	Dk. Green	Purple Crimson	Large	Double	Yes	Very	Yes	Yes	Yes
HARVEST HOME	5 x 5	Lt. Green	Mauve Pink	Large	Semi-Dbl.	Some	Some	Yes		
HENRY HUDSON	4 x 3	Sm. Dk. Green	White	Medium	Semi-Dbl.	Yes	Yes	Yes	Yes	No
HOLLANDICA	7 x 7	Deep Green	Deep Pink	Large	Single	Yes	Yes	Yes	Yes	Yes
HUNTER	4 x 3	Dk. Green	Bright Red	Medium	Double	Yes	Yes	Yes	Yes	
IWARA	Vigorous		White	Small	Single	No		Yes		
JENS MUNK	5 x 5	Sm. Med. Green	Bright Pink	Medium	Semi-Dbl.	Yes	Yes	Yes	Yes	Some
KAMTCHATICA	7 x 6	Medium Green	Deep Pink	Small	Single	No	Yes	Yes	Yes	Yes
LADY CURZON	4 x 6	Deep Olive Green	Pale Pink	Large	Single	No	Yes	Quite	Yes	No
LADY DUNCAN	2 x 6	Glossy	Bright Pink	Large	Single	No		Yes	Yes	
LE CID	Vigorous		Bright Crimson							Some
LINDA CAMPBELL	5 x 8	Medium Green	Deep Crimson	Large	Semi-Dbl.	Yes		Yes	Yes	
MME. GEORGES BRUANT	5 x 4	Dark Green	White	Large	Semi-Dbl.	Yes	Yes	Yes	Yes	Some
MME. JULIEN POTIN	4 x 4	Leathery	Flesh Pink	Large	Double	Yes	Yes	Tender	Some	
MARIE BUGNET	3 x 3	Elongated	White	Large	Double	Yes	Yes	Yes	Yes	No
MARTIN FROBISHER	5 x 4	Gray Green	Pale Pink	Medium	Double	Yes	Light	Yes	Yes	No
MARY MANNERS	4 x 3	Dark Green	White	Large	Double	Yes	Yes	Yes	Some	No
MAX GRAF	2 x 8	Glossy Dark Green	Clear Pink	Large	Single	No	Yes	Yes	Yes	Seldom
MICRUGOSA	5 x 4	Elongated	Pale Pink	Large	Single		Yes			Yes

NAME	SIZE	FOLIAGE	BLOSSOM COLOR	BLOSSOM SIZE	BLOSSOM TYPE	RECURRENT	FRAGRANT	HARDY	DISEASE RESISTANT	HIPS
MICRUGOSA ALBA	5 x 4	Elongated	White	Large	Single		Yes			Yes
MRS. ANTHONY WATERER	4 x 5	Dark Green	Deep Crimson	Medium	Double	Yes	Very	Quite	Some	No
MRS. JOHN MCNAB	5 x 5	Gray Green	Blush Pink	Medium	Semi-Dbl.	No	Yes	Very	Very	
MOJE HAMMARBERG	4 x 4	Dark Green	Purple Crimson	Large	Double	Yes	Yes	Yes	Yes	Yes
NIGEL HAWTHORNE	Low spreading	Glossy	Salmon-Pink	Medium	Single		Light	?		Sparse
NOVA ZEMBLA	6 x 5	Lg. Dk. Green	Blush White	Large	Double	Yes	Yes	Quite	Some	No
NYVELDT'S WHITE	5 x 4	Light Green	White	Large	Single	Yes	Yes	Yes	Yes	Yes
R. x PAULII	3 x 8	Dark Green	White	Large	Single	No	Yes	Yes	Yes	Yes
PINK GROOTENDORST	5 x 4	Sm. Lt. Green	Bright Pink	Small	Double	Yes	No	Yes	Some	No
PIRETTE PAVEMENT	3 x 3	Deep Green	Light Pink	Medium	Semi-double	Yes	Yes	Yes	Yes	Yes
PRAIRIE MAID	4 x 4	Decorative	Cream	Medium	Double	Some	Yes	Yes	Yes	
PURPLE PAVEMENT	3 x 3	Deep Green	Purple Crimson	Medium	Semi-Dbl.	Yes	Yes	Yes	Yes	Yes
RHEINAUPARK	4 x 4	Dark Green	Scarlet	Large	Semi-Dbl.	Yes	Light	Quite	Some	
ROBUSTA	5 x 4	Dark Green	Scarlet	Large	Single	Yes	Light	Quite	Some	No
ROSE Á PARFUM DE L'HAŸ	4 x 4	Deep Green	Purple Red	Large	Semi-Dbl.	Yes	Very	Quite	Some	Some
ROSERAIE DE L' HAŸ	6 x 5	Dark Green	Purple Crimson	Large	Semi-Dbl.	Yes	Very	Yes	Yes	Some
RÖTE MAX GRAF	2 x 8	Glossy Dark Green	Medium Red	Large	Single	No	Yes	Yes	Yes	Seldom
RUGELDA	5 x 4	Leathery	Lemon-Yellow	Medium	Semi-Dbl.	Yes	Yes	Quite		
RUGOSA MAGNIFICA	4 x 5	Dark Green	Purple Crimson	Large	Double	Yes	Yes	Yes	Yes	Yes
R. x RUGOTIDA	3 x 4	Glossy Elongated	Pink		Single			Yes	Yes	No
RUGSPIN		Dark Green	Wine Crimson	Large	Single	Yes	Yes	Yes	Yes	Yes
RUSKIN	4 x 5	Medium Green	Crimson Red	Large	Double	Some	Very	Tender		No
SARAH VAN FLEET	5 x 4	Glossy, Bright Green	Med. Pink	Large	Semi-Dbl.	Yes	Yes	Yes	Yes	No
SCABROSA	6 x 4	Lg. Dk. Green	Crimson Pink	Large	Single	Yes	Yes	Yes	Yes	Yes
SCHNEELICHT	6 x 6	Medium Green	White	Large	Single	No	Yes	Yes	Yes	
SCHNEEZWERG	4 x 4	Dark Green	White	Medium	Semi-Dbl.	Yes	Yes	Yes	Yes	Yes
SIGNE RELANDER	6 x 5	Dark Green	Dark Red	Small	Double	Yes	Some			

NAME	SIZE	FOLIAGE	BLOSSOM COLOR	BLOSSOM SIZE	BLOSSOM TYPE	RECURRENT	FRAGRANT	HARDY	DISEASE RESISTANT	HIPS
SIMONET'S	6 x 5		Pink	Medium	Double	No	Yes	Yes		
SIR THOMAS LIPTON	6 x 5	Dark Green	White	Large	Double	Some	Yes	Quite	Some	No
SNOW PAVEMENT	3 x 3	Deep Green	White	Medium	Semi-double	Yes	Yes	Yes	Yes	Yes
SOUVENIR DE PHILÉMON COCHET	5 x 4	Dark Green	White	Large	Double	Yes	Yes	Yes	Yes	No
STAR DELIGHT	2 x 2	Small	Bright Pink	Small	Single	Yes				
THÉRÈSE BUGNET	5 x 4	Gray Green	Pink	Large	Double	Yes	Yes	Yes	Yes	
THUSNELDA	6 x 6		Medium Pink	Large	Semi-Dbl.	No	Yes			
TOPAZ JEWEL	5 x 7	Dark Green	Pale Yellow	Large	Semi-Dbl.	Yes	Some		Some	No
VANGUARD	8 x 6	Lg. Glossy Dark Green	Salmon	Large	Double	Yes	Yes	Tender	Some	
WASAGAMING	6 x 6	Deep Green	Medium Pink	Large	Double	Yes	Yes	Yes		
WEISSE MAX GRAF	2 x 8	Glossy Dark Green	White	Large	Semi-Dbl.	No	Yes	Yes	Yes	Seldom
WHITE GROOTENDORST	4 x 4	Light Green	White	Small	Double	Yes	No	Yes	Some	No
WILL ALDERMAN	4 x 4	Dark Green	Lilac Pink	Large	Double	Yes	Very	Yes	Yes	
YELLOW FRU DAGMAR	4 x 4		Yellow	Large	Double	Yes		?		No

Bibliography

American Rose Society, comp. *Modern Roses 8: The International Check-list of Roses*. Edited by Catherine E. Meikle. Harrisburg, Pa.: McFarland Co., 1980.

——. *Modern Roses 9: The International Checklist of Roses In Cultivation or of Historical or Botanical Importance*. Edited by P. A. Haring. Shreveport, La.: The American Rose Society, 1986.

Austin, David. *The Heritage of the Rose*. Woodbridge: Antique Collectors' Club, 1988.

Beales, Peter. *Classic Roses*. New York: Henry Holt & Company, 1985.

——. *Twentieth-Century Roses*. New York: Harper & Row, Publishers, 1988.

Crow, J. W. "Breeding Roses for Canada." Simcoe, Ontario. n.d. Photocopy.

Darlington, H. R. "Rugosa Roses." *Journal of the International Garden Club* (Baltimore, Md.) 1, no. 1 (1917): 219–35.

Epping, Jeffrey E. and Dr. Edward R. Hasselkus. "Spotlight on Shrub Roses." *American Nurseryman*, July 15, 1989, 27–39.

Griffiths, Trevor. *The Book of Old Roses*. London: Michael Joseph, 1984.

——. *The Book of Classic Old Roses*. London: Michael Joseph, 1987.

——. *A Celebration of Old Roses*. London: Michael Joseph, 1990.

Jekyll, Gertrude and Edward Mawley. *Roses for English Gardens*. Woodbridge: Antique Collectors' Club, 1982.

Krüssmann, Gerd. *The Complete Book of Roses*. Translated by G. K. and Nigel Raban. Portland, Oreg.: Timber Press, 1981.

——. *Manual of Cultivated Broad-Leaved Trees & Shrubs*. 3 vols. Translated by Michael E. Epp, and edited by Gilbert S. Daniels. Portland, Oreg.: Timber Press, 1985–1986.

Le Rougetel, Hazel. *A Heritage of Roses*. Owings Mill, Md.: Stemmer House, 1988.

Osborne, Robert. *Roses for Canadian Gardens*. Toronto: Key Porter Books, 1991.

Phillips, Roger, and Martyn Rix. *Roses*. New York: Random House, 1988.

Scanniello, Stephen, and Tania Bayard. *Roses of America*. New York: Henry Holt & Company, Donald Hutter Book, 1990.

Shepherd, Roy E. *History of the Rose*. 1954 Facsimile reprint. New York: Earl M. Coleman, 1978.

Skinner, F. L. *Horticultural Horizons*. Winnipeg: Manitoba Department of Agriculture & Conservation, 1966.

Thomas, Graham Stuart. *Shrub Roses of Today*. rev. ed. London: J. M. Dent & Sons, 1962.

——. ed. *A Garden of Roses: Watercolours by Alfred Parsons, RA*. Topsfield, Mass.: Salem House Publishers, 1987.

Plant Source Publications

Combined Rose List, a yearly listing of roses in commerce and cultivation and where to find them. Compiled and available from: Beverly R. Dobson, 215 Harriman Road, Irvington, NY 10533.

Andersen Horticultural Library's Source List of Plants and Seeds: A Completely Revised Listing of 1988–89 Catalogues, Compiled by Richard T. Isaacson, a listing of sources for over 40,000 plants commercially available in North America. Available from: Andersen Horticultural Library, Minnesota Landscape Arboretum, Box 39, Chanhassen, MN 55317.

Rose Specialists

SOURCES AND RESOURCES

Canada

Corn Hill Nursery, Ltd.
RR 5, Petitcodiac
New Brunswick Canada
  E0A 2H0
Free catalog
(506) 756-3635

Hortico, Inc.
RR 1, Waterdown
Ontario Canada L0R 2H0
Catalog $2
(416) 689-6984

Pickering Nurseries, Inc.
670 Kingston Road
Pickering, Ontario
Canada L1V 1A6
Catalog $2
(416) 839-2111

Roseberry Gardens
Box 933, Thunder Bay
Ontario Canada P7C 4X8
Catalog $1
  ($100 minimum US customers)

USA

Antique Rose Emporium
Route 5, Box 143
Brenham, TX 77833
Catalog $2
(409) 836-9051

Forevergreen Farm
70 New Gloucester Road
North Yarmouth, ME 04021
Free catalog
(207) 829-5830

Heirloom Old Garden Roses
24062 Riverside Drive NE
St. Paul, OR 97137
Free catalog
(503) 538-1576

Heritage Rosarium
211 Haviland Mill Road
Brookeville, MD 20833-2311
List $1
(301) 774-2806

High Country Rosarium
1717 Downing Street
Denver, CO 80218
Catalog $1
(303) 832-4026

Lowe's own-root Roses
6 Sheffield Road
Nashua, NH 03062
Catalog $2
(603) 888-2214

Sequoia Nursery
2519 East Noble
Visalia, CA 93277
Free catalog
(209) 732-0190

Valley Nursery
P.O. Box 4845
2801 North Montana Avenue
Free catalog
Helena, MT 59604
(406) 442-8460

England

David Austin Roses
Bowling Green Lane
Albrighton, Wolverhampton
England WV7 3HB

Peter Beales Roses
London Road, Attelborough,
  Norfolk
England NR17 1AY

Germany

W. Kordes' Sohne
2206 Klein Offenseth
Sparrieshoop, Germany

To obtain permit to import roses write:

Permit Unit
United States Department
  of Agriculture
Plant Protection and
  Quarantine Programs
Federal Building, Room 632
6505 Belcrest Road
Hyattsville, MD 20782

Societies

American Rose Society
Membership Secretary
P.O. Box 30,000
Shreveport, LA 71130
(318) 938-5407

Heritage Rose Group
Mr. Charles A. Walker
1512 Gorman Street
Raleigh, NC 27606

SUZANNE VERRIER has written and illustrated *Titus Tidewater* and is the illustrator of five other children's books. She currently owns and operates Forevergreen Farm nursery, selling old-fashioned, uncommon, and hardy roses both locally and by mail order. Verrier also lectures on the subject of old-fashioned roses. She lives and gardens in North Yarmouth, Maine.

CHARLES STEINHACKER is an award-winning landscape and conservation photographer whose books include *Superior: Portrait of a Living Lake*, *Yellowstone: A Century of the Wilderness Idea*, and *The Sand Country of Aldo Leopold* (Sierra Club). His work has appeared in *National Geographic*, *Life*, *Audubon*, and other periodicals. Steinhacker's photographs have been widely exhibited. He has taught photography throughout the country.